WHAT A TIME TO LIVE

JAMES B. HAMILTON, 1933-1994

WHAT A TIME TO LIVE

The Autobiography of

James B. Hamilton

Michigan State University
East Lansing
1995

© 1995 Michigan State University

Distributed for Michigan State University by Michigan State University Press.

This book is produced on paper that meets requirements of the American National Standard of Information Sciences—Permanence of paper for printed materials, ANSI Z23.48-1984.

Printed in the United States of America

Distributed by Michigan State University Press
East Lansing, Michigan 48823-5202

02 01 00 99 98 97 96 95 1 2 3 4 5 6 7 8 9 10

Library of Congress Cataloging-in Publication Data

Hamilton, James B., 1933-1994.
   What a time to live : the autobiography of James B. Hamilton.
         p.   c.m.
   Includes biographical references.
   ISBN 0-87013-353-5
   1. Hamilton, James B., 1933-1994. 2. Chemists—United States—Biography. 3. Afro-American chemists—Biography. 4. Educators—United States—Biography. 5. Amyotrophic lateral sclerosis—Patients—United States—Biography. I. Title
CT275.H2897A3 1995
540.9'2—dc20
[B]
                                                                                    95-46
                                                                                     CIP

To Ruth, Bramlett, and Priscilla
for their love and support

Dawn to Dusk

Love can be like a waking thought.
You sense it, smooth as a silken sheet.
Your soul drinks in the warmth as it
      spreads across your body and your
      mind.
You strive to recapture that fleeting touch
      . . . reach just a little further
"Is it there? What is within my grasp?"

You wonder.

Dreams move into reality. Love peers out
      at you.
Walking, a breeze strokes the surface of
      your skin. . . you freeze.
Your spirit, seeking drink, causes you to
      shiver with beautiful memories.
You turn full circle, searching for the
      source of your happiness.
"Nothing/no one is there! Are you
      scared?"

You wonder.

Love is still with you as dreams return.
The dream returns like a ghostly hand
      tracing your spirit like the air
      which enfolds you.
Your soul stretches with liquid stealth.
Shivering you enter the spirit world of the
      dream.
You cannot capture this, but you can taste
      it.
      . . . enthralled in its presence
"Are you real? Am I alone?"

You wonder.

You realize the answer truly does not
      matter.
The love is there.

Priscilla Simms Hamilton

What a time
to live,
to love,
to laugh,
to cry,
and at day's end
to view the
setting sun
with a sigh.

J. B. Hamilton
1964

CONTENTS

PREFACE

This book has had a most interesting evolution. It is my own autobiography, but I approached the task only with substantial urging from the person to whom I reported at Michigan State University, Provost David K. Scott. Thus, at the outset I must acknowledge David Scott's encouragement. I took the idea and ran with it. The book is autobiographical, consisting of ten chapters. Chapter one (Childhood, Family, Schooling, and Friends) is concerned with my early life in Chicago, Illinois, my employment opportunities, and my years in the Marine Corps. There I talk about family, friends, and experiences that had a major influence upon my life. I also describe in some detail my extended family and their importance to me. This chapter, concerned as it is with my early growth and development, should appeal to many readers, but it should prove most interesting to young people growing up today, particularly those about to embark upon a higher education experience and who are the first in their family to have such an experience. Because I am an African American citizen, this chapter of the book should also have a special interest to young and old African Americans.

The reader will note that I have made a conscious decision to use the term "African American" instead of "Black" or "Afro-American." When the story begins the term in use was "Negro" or "Colored." At Iowa State University in the 1960s the designation changed to "Black" or "Afro-American." I decided to make use of the term "African American" in the text after careful reflection on the dominant current custom. I do, however, occasionally fall back into the use of Black. In addition, because in this book emphasis is placed upon the African American experience in a predominantly white society and in predominantly white universities, I have chosen to identify individuals and groups by their racial background.

Chapter two (Undergraduate College and University Days and the Woman of My Life) addresses my early experiences with higher education, leading ultimately to my attainment of the Master of Science degree in chemistry from Northwestern University, Evanston, Illinois. This chapter also describes my adult life in the period where I began to take seriously what my role and contribution might be in the society. I, for example, meet my future spouse at this time. The bulk of the section, however, is concerned with my experiences at the University of Illinois, Northwestern University (in Chicago), and Northwestern University (in Evanston). There is also a small section on the impact of an employment experience at IIT Research Institute while I was attending Northwestern University. This chapter also addresses my experiences at Morton Chemical Company.

Chapter three (African American Ph.D. Production at Iowa State University) addresses my experiences at Iowa State University, where I earned a Ph.D. degree in chemistry and had a range of different other growth experiences. My son was born in Iowa, and the chapter primarily focuses on a young African American family making its start in middle America. The period of graduate study and what was happening at Iowa State at this time should prove interesting. Chapter three, because it is concerned with the period during which I did my undergraduate and graduate work at three different universities, should be of interest to young people about to embark upon a higher education experience at either the undergraduate or graduate level. I stress the importance of mentoring in this chapter because faculty mentors were such an integral part of my educational development.

Chapters four through ten, which make up the bulk of this autobiography, share my experiences at Michigan State University from 1968-1993. These 25 years comprise what I believe has been a unique period in the history of this university, and you hear it from the perspective of a male African American professor who begins his journey at MSU as a postdoctoral research associate in chemistry and continues to become a professor and university administrator. This period includes the era within which the population of African American, Asian American, Hispanic, and Native American students grew significantly at undergraduate, graduate-professional, and graduate levels. It is an era about which little has been written and in which many should have considerable interest. I address such significant events as the growth and transformation of academic support services for undergraduates at Michigan State University during this period, the rise and fall of the College of Urban Development, and the establishment of the Black Faculty and Administrators Association. Two major student demonstrations occurred, and I discuss both: (1) the 1969 Wilson Hall incident, a major African American student demonstration, and (2) two decades later the occupation of the Hannah Administration Building by African American students.

My daughter, Priscilla, was born in 1971. I describe the African naming ceremony held for her that year.

The Council to Review Undergraduate Education receives considerable attention, and details provide an inside look at the emergence of recommendations from the 1987-88 review of undergraduate education at Michigan State University.

While telling my story, I try to keep in order the flow of events to make reading easy. If I have not been successful, the fault is all mine.

▼

ACKNOWLEDGMENTS

I would like to acknowledge the contributions of many who have made this book possible. Of course, without Viciki Dukelow, my executive staff assistant—who not only typed this manuscript from dictated tapes but also assisted in its editing—this book would never have appeared. My spouse, Professor Ruth Simms Hamilton; John A. Hannah Professor Darlene Clark Hine; and my editors provided invaluable assistance by carefully reading this manuscript. Professor John Greene has also provided invaluable assistance. I also wish to acknowledge the special editing by Elizabeth Johnston, and the assistance with editing provided by Delores Reed, Suseann VanLiew, Carol Milliman, Jan King, Chris Reist, and, of course, my able students Kevin Summey and Ursula Phoenix. Beyond this I called upon people external to the university, such as Clark Chipman; George Jackson; my mother, Maude Posey; my wife, Ruth Simms Hamilton; and my children, Bramlett and Priscilla, all of whom agreed to read the manuscript at various stages of completion. Finally, I am personally responsible for the current form and the contents of this book.

▼

PROLOGUE

M y arrival at Michigan State University was the beginning of my 25-year career in higher education. I had not planned at the beginning of my graduate study in chemistry to go into higher education; nonetheless, by the time I completed it I found higher education to be an attractive option. I also came to discover that Michigan State University was an excellent place to pursue such a career. When I arrived on the MSU campus, President John A. Hannah was ending his long and distinguished career. The country and the university were recovering from a series of national disasters that included the assassinations of John F. Kennedy, Robert F. Kennedy, Martin Luther King, Jr., Malcolm X, Medgar Evers, and others, which followed on the heels of the modern the Civil Rights movement, and a major period of discontent that emerged in reaction to the nation's continuing involvement in Vietnam. In response to a racial crisis in the State of Michigan following riots in Detroit and other major cities in the Lower Peninsula, President Hannah appointed a group known as "the Committee of Sixteen," The committee recommended the creation of a Center for Racial and Urban Affairs to guide MSU into a new era of campus accessibility for African Americans and other racial minorities. Hannah left MSU at the end of 1968, my first year, to become head of the U.S. Civil Rights Commission in Washington, DC. Walter Adams, professor of economics, who was highly respected at MSU and across the state, succeded Hannah as the university's president.

As president, Walter Adams was a strong advocate both for faculty and students. During his tenure, and my second year, issues regarding MSU's future and its response to African Americans and other racial minorities continued to be a major concern requiring presidential attention. Two major demonstrations by African Americans and African students occurred during Walter Adams's tenure and led to new commitments to expand access for African American students, faculty, staff, and administrators at MSU. During President Adams's tenure, the search began for a new president for Michigan State University. And even though I was just a new faculty member trying to make a home in the Department of Chemistry, I inevitably found myself drawn into discussions of the issues confronting the university. Dr. Robert L. Green, professor of education, became a principal reason for my being drawn into these events. In his role as director of the Center for Urban Affairs, Green worked to insure the academic success of African American students who were beginning to enroll at Michigan State University in increasing numbers by 1969. Professor Green was involved in a project known as the Detroit Geographical Expeditionary Institute (DGEI), which took a committed group of faculty members into the city of Detroit to teach Black students so that they might be better prepared to attend MSU. Two others involved with the project were Dr. Eileen VanTassell of the Department of Natural Science, and Dr. John J. Masterson of the Department of Mathematics. The DGEI led to a new admissions program called The Detroit Project and later the Developmental Program.

The presidential search ended with the selection of an African American, Clifton R. Wharton, Jr., as Michigan State University's 14th president. This turn of events I had not anticipated, but Wharton's presence would be a major incentive for my remaining at MSU. President Clifton Wharton and his wife, Dolores, began a new era at MSU. Among other things, President Wharton saw the need immediately to set MSU on a new direction in the recruitment, admission, and enrollment of a more diverse student body. One of his first acts was to create the President's Commission on Admissions and Student Body Composition. I became one of many from the MSU community—which included alumni, faculty, students, and friends of the university—to serve on this historic body. Ultimately it produced a report containing recommendations that focused on the need for MSU to be more accessible to various student groups, including adults, handicappers, the disadvantaged, and minorities. The recommendations focused, not only on undergraduates, but also on graduate education and, of course, on those involved with lifelong education. I worked on that commission with deep feelings within me for the need to have a broader picture of what this university was about. I met a large group of people because of my work on that commission, and, as a result, I would ultimately join the Office of the Provost, where I worked for over twenty years under five different provosts, beginning in 1971 with John E. Cantlon and ending in the 1990s with Lou Anna K. Simon. All those years would find me exspending my energy seeking to carry out the agenda laid out by President Wharton's Commission on Admissions and Student Body Composition as it related to disadvantaged students, handicapper students, and minority students.

President Clifton Wharton gave Michigan State University a new visibility on the national level, in part because he was an effective leader, an African American, and also because he represented the eastern elites, having attended Boston Latin School and Harvard University before earning his Ph.D. in agricultural economics at the University of Chicago. He and his wife, Dolores, would have a long-term relationship with the university, unlike that of any other in the recent past, except that of John A. Hannah. They returned to MSU often after they left the campus in 1977 to help the university in various ways, including raising funds for a new Performing Arts Center that ultimately would be named after them. In addition, they came back to the campus for the inauguration of new presidents; to receive honors, including honorary degrees and presidential medallions; and for other events.

President Wharton was followed in succession by presidents Edgar Harden, Cecil Mackey, John A. DiBiaggio, Gordon Guyer, and M. Peter McPherson. Each in his own way would have an impact on the university as it moved toward realization of its long-term mission. These years, however, were marked by budgetary constraints in Michigan. Efforts to deal with fiscal problems plagued the tenure of President Mackey. Under President DiBiaggio there would be a brief respite, but budget problems would reemerge toward the end of his tenure, as well. By the time Gordon Guyer assumed the presidency,

MSU faced a new state of fiscal crisis (undeclared)—almost equivalent to, or worse, than the one experienced in 1980.

Michigan State University rose from being primarily an agricultural college during the early days of President Hannah's administration to become a major AAU and land-grant research institution with a commitments to graduate, undergraduate, and continuing education. It received NSF "Centers of Excellence" grants in the College of Natural Science, and under President Hannah it completed a major building campaign that transformed it into one of the largest single-campus universities in the United States. MSU also attracted a distinguished faculty from the best-known and most respected universities in the nation. All hoped and expected that MSU would continue to grow. There were, however, those within the university who continued to see the land-grant mission and the commitment to the education of undergraduates in the State of Michigan as the primary and continuing role for the institution For my entire quarter of a century here, there was a continuing tension between these desires. A reality for MSU has been that it is the largest undergraduate institution in the entire state, and over 90 percent of its undergraduate population are residents of Michigan. Undergraduate education continues to be a major part of the MSU mission, even as the university's stature in graduate education, research, and lifelong education has grown and evolved.

Michigan State University is now poised at the end of a major period of expansion and change. It confronts new fiscal challenges, and the direction of its future growth and development are not yet certain. In addition, a new generation of administrators and faculty is entering the university and will assume responsibility for deciding its future path. As I reflect upon my 25 years at MSU, I remain confident that the university will transcend the whatever adversities it may confront and that itt and survive as one of the nation's preeminent land-grant and AAU institutions. I have been proud to be a part of its faculty and its administration, and I enjoyed every one of the years that I was a part of this community. They were not been dull or boring. They were always interesting and challenging. Somehow, I cannot help but marvel that my early days in Chicago, when I played with a little chemistry set, put me on my path toward higher education, a path that would lead to East Lansing, Michigan, and Michigan State University.

CHRONOLOGY

1933	▼	James B Hamilton born in Chicago, Illinois.
1940s to 1951	▼	Attended elementary and high school in Chicago, Illinois.
1951	▼	Aborted attempt to study at Herzl Community College in Chicago.
1951-53	▼	Employment at America Fore Insurance Company, Commonwealth Edison Company, and Western Electric Corporation in Chicago.
1953-56	▼	U.S. Marines, including a 1954 tour of duty in Korea.
1956	▼	Discharged from the U.S. Marine Corps.
1957	▼	Attended the University of Illinois at the Navy Pier, Chicago, Illinois.
1959	▼	Began a two-year employment as chemical technician at IIT Research Institute (formerly Armour Research Foundation) and began night school at the evening division branch of Northwestern University in Chicago, Illinois.
1961	▼	Earned a bachelor of philosophy degree with a major in chemistry from Northwestern University.
	▼	Continued study for the master's degree in chemistry at Northwestern University in Evanston, Illinois.

1963	▼	Completed study for a master's degree in chemistry at Northwestern University at Evanston, Illinois, and began employment as a research chemist at Morton Chemical Company in Woodstock, Illinois.
1964	▼	Began study for a Ph.D. in chemistry at Iowa State University in Ames, Iowa.
1965	▼	Became engaged to, and subsequently married Ruth Priscilla Simms in Savannah, Georgia, on July 3, 1965.
1966	▼	Traveled west with wife on a camping trip to the Tetons and Yellowstone National Park in Wyoming, taking sailboat.
1967	▼	African American students began protest at Iowa State University.
1967	▼	Ruth and James were blessed by the birth of son Bramlett Wendell Hamilton on November 28, 1967, in Ames, Iowa.
1968	▼	The Hamiltons moved into their new residence in East Lansing, Michigan, and began employment at Michigan State University.
1969	▼	Hamilton accepted a tenure-track position as an assistant professor in Michigan State University's Department of Chemistry.
	▼	African American students initiated major sit-in and protest at MSU's Wilson Hall cafeteria.
	▼	Hamilton appointed by President Walter Adams to a committee to investigate Wilson Hall affair.
1970	▼	Clifton R. Wharton, Jr., became president of Michigan State University, the first African American president of a major, predominantly white, university.
1971	▼	Hamilton assumed additional responsibilities as assistant provost for Special Programs at Michigan State University.
	▼	Ruth and James Hamilton were blessed with a second child, Priscilla Simms Hamilton, born to them on August 26, 1971, in Lansing, Michigan.

1972	▼	In December 1972 James Hamilton and his son, Bramlett, accompanied Ruth on a seven-week visit to London and to West Africa.
1975	▼	Experienced a grievance hearing following the firing of an assistant director who reported to him.
1976	▼	Continued teaching and research in chemistry and administrative duties as assistant provost, and assumed additional responsibility as assistant dean of The Graduate School.
	▼	Larry Boger became provost for Michigan State University for a brief period. Lee Winder assumed duties as associate provost.
1976	▼	Christine Wilson assumed responsibility for a reorganized Office of Supportive Services.
1977	▼	Wharton resigned; Edgar Harden was appointed interim president.
	▼	Christine Wilson resigned as director of the Office of Supportive Services.
	▼	Florence Harris was appointed assistant director of the Office of Supportive Services.
1979	▼	Cecil Mackey was appointed president of Michigan State University.
	▼	Hamilton left Michigan State University to direct a program at Argonne National Laboratory.
1980	▼	Hamilton returned to MSU as assistant provost for Undergraduate Education in July.
1981	▼	University experienced 6.2% decline in undergraduate enrollment and establishes task forces to study problems.
1982	▼	William Turner appointed director of the Office of Admissions and Scholarships.
	▼	Hamilton received American Chemical Society's Henry A. Hill Lectureship Award.

1984	▼	Hamilton visited East and West Africa as a representative of National Science Foundation.
1985	▼	Hamilton visited West Africa to participate in an international conference on science and technology jointly sponsored by AAAS and ASCI.
	▼	Cecil Mackey resigned as MSU president; John A. DiBiaggio assumed presidency of Michigan State University.
1986	▼	Hamilton participated in Harvard University Institute on Educational Management.
	▼	David K. Scott assumed position as provost and vice president for Academic Affairs at Michigan State University.
	▼	Hamilton and staff participated in the First International Conference on the Freshman Year Experience, held in Southhampton, England.
1987	▼	Hamilton participated in Second International Conference on the Freshman Year Experience in Cambridge, England.
	▼	University undertakes the review of undergraduate education.
1988	▼	The Report of the Council to Review Undergraduate Education was completed, and implementation of the report begins.
1989	▼	Parents of African American students protested at Michigan State University and met with President John DiBiaggio.
	▼	African American students occupied Hannah Administration Building lobby to protest racist conditions at Michigan State University.
1989	▼	Bramlett graduated from MSU; Priscilla graduated from Okemos High School.
	▼	Bramlett began study at Stanford University Law School, and Priscilla began undergraduate study at Stanford.
	▼	Confirmation received that Hamilton has the disease amyotrophic lateral sclerosis, or Lou Gehrig's Disease.

▼ All the support programs, including the Office of Supportive Services and the Office of Programs for Handicapper Students, as well as Upward Bound, the Foreign TA Orientation Program, and the Martin Luther King, Jr.-Cesar Chavez-Rosa Parks College Day Program, were placed under the responsibility of Lonnie Eiland, director of the Undergraduate University Division.

▼ Plans were made to relocate all support programs in Bessey Hall.

▼ John Greene, an African American, was appointed director of the Office of Integrative Studies.

1990 ▼ The Mid-America Association of Educational Opportunity Program Personnel honored Hamilton with a special recognition program at the spring meeting of the association held in Chicago, Illinois, at the McCormick Center Hotel.

▼ Hamilton visited Costa Rica with his wife, Ruth, and graduate students from the African Diaspora Research Program.

1991 ▼ ALS continued to have its impact upon Hamilton. He entered the hospital in the spring, underwent a tracheotomy and is fitted with a trach and a machine—a ventilator—to breathe for him.

▼ Hamilton returned to work as consultant to the provost after resigning his position as assistant provost for Undergraduate Education.

▼ Provost Scott developed plan for reorganizing the Office of the Provost, particularly Hamilton's area.

1992 ▼ Hamilton completed planning for a CIC Conference on Retention, and the conference is held at Michigan State University, February 23-25.

▼ Representatives of the Black Faculty and Administrators Association (BFAA) met with members of the MSU Board of Trustees and with President DiBiaggio and Provost Scott to protest lack of action in response to their requests.

1992 ▼ President DiBiaggio announced his decision to accept the presidency at Tufts, effective September 1, 1992. The Board of Trustees appointed Gordon Guyer as interim president.

▼ Following President DiBiaggio's resignation, Provost Scott decided to step down as provost of Michigan State University, making his announcement in August 1992. President Guyer appointed Lou Anna K. Simon as interim provost.

▼ Hamilton arranged, through the efforts of his wife, to go to California to observe the graduation of son, Bramlett, from Stanford Law School.

▼ The Board of Trustees began the search for a new MSU president.

▼ Asian-American and Latino undergraduates complained to the vice president for Student Affairs (VPSA) about the distribution of funds to minority groups by the Office of Minority Affairs (OMA).

▼ Lack of adequate response by OMA and the VPSA led to a larger protest to President Guyer and to the Board of Trustees.

▼ Statewide elections changed the membership of the Board of Trustees with the addition of two Democrats (Dorothy Gonzales and Bob Traxler).

1993 ▼ David Scott accepted position as chancellor at the University of Massachusetts at Amherst.

▼ President Guyer responded to demands of Asian-American and Latino undergraduates by transferring the Office of Minority Affairs and the Office of Financial Aids from the vice president for Student Affairs to the assistant provost for Student Academic Support Services and Racial, Ethnic, and Multicultural Issues.

▼ African American and Latino undergraduates sponsored a conference on campus to resolve differences.

▼ The Board of Trustees announced on-campus interviews of candidate M. Peter McPherson on August 17; he is appointed 19th president of MSU on the same day. He began his tenure as president on October 1.

1994 ▼ James B. Hamilton died, May 18.

▼ Priscilla graduated from Stanford University, June 12.

▼

CHAPTER ONE

CHILDHOOD, FAMILY, SCHOOLING, & FRIENDS

I was born in Chicago, Illinois, on October 22, 1933, the son of Howard and Maude Hamilton. I knew my father well, but he died in 1946, the year I turned 13. My older brother, Howard Hamilton, Jr., died of a fall in 1975. My widowed mother and my maternal grandparents, with whom we stayed, raised Howard and me. My mother worked full time to provide support. Our small family had close linkages with a much larger extended family in Chicago, which had roots in Kentucky, and with other branches in Springfield, Illinois, and Indianapolis, Indiana. This was on my mother's side of the family. When I grew up in Chicago I had numerous cousins with whom I was very close, as close as a sibling. Some of us were within one year of one another in age.

My mother's sister Kay, her husband, Percy, and their five children—Katherine, Maurice, Jeannette, Jenola, and Doris Jean—all lived on the west side of Chicago. I particularly enjoyed Uncle Percy, who built several new business enterprises. In my younger days he ran a jitney or cab service.

Another favorite, Aunt Mary (who was called "Dimple"), married Otto Lawrence. They had 12 children: Mary, Al, Carl, Jean, Michael, Delores, Ricky, Wanda, Rita, Brenda, Joyce, and Janice. The Lawrence's lived in the Ida B. Wells Development, which was one of the earlier and more modern projects built in Chicago back in the 1930s. Since that time the facility has gone downhill; most new projects do not measure up to the quality of the old Ida B. Wells.

Aunt Morabelle married Fred McClinton, who operated a milk route when I was a child. Later, Fred joined with his brother to purchase a grocery store and stayed in that business for the rest of his life. Morabelle and Fred lived not far from us when I was growing up; they were a great family. They had two sons—Fred, Jr., and David and two daughters, Sandra and Madeline. I babysat for the daughters a lot, particularly in the 1940s, when Fred was away in the Army. I bribed them to call me "uncle." At 13 I felt I was old enough to be an uncle, and I wanted to have that status. The idea of bribing them with gifts came from my mother, who had done the same thing with me as a child to get me to call her Mother, instead of Maude. Morabelle was not the youngest aunt, however. Mother's youngest sister was Christine, married to James Crooks, with whom she had James and Emmanita.

Uncle James Jones, my mother's only brother, married Sarah and raised two sons, Leslie and Darryl. They, too, lived on the south side of the city, and I often spent a great deal of time at their home. James and Sarah enjoyed cooking and entertaining the family. As I grew older, I would regularly visit them, as James was the elder male to whom I had become very close when we lived together during my youth. I still think of James almost as a second brother. Sarah was a thoroughly wonderful and outgoing person who loved to work. She is a nurse and once served as the private duty nurse for the late mayor of Chicago, Richard J. Daley.

I take the time to talk about my aunts and uncles and their families because I saw them as such an important part of my growing up in Chicago. We would get together as a large family several times a year. Not uncommonly, we had family picnics together in the summer. There was a regular stud poker game that I observed as a child in which my aunts and uncles and other cousins participated. Hardly a month went by that they did not have a game at someone's home; it usually lasted most of the night. Conflict never arose, and no one got upset as the result of someone's winning or losing in this table stake or pot limit game. I watched regularly as a young child, joined the game when I turned nineteen, and continued to play poker into my adult life.

My maternal grandparents, James Leslie Jones (1885-1965) and Emma Nelson Jones (1889-1985) headed this large, wonderful family. Both were born on farms in Kentucky, not far from Louisville. My grandparents migrated to Springfield, Illinois, in the early 1900s and were there in 1908, when the big race riot occurred. My mother was born in Springfield in 1910. During or shortly after World War I the family migrated to Chicago, Illinois, where they stayed.

My paternal grandmother, Alice Foster, and her few relatives came from St. Louis, Missouri, to Chicago, where my father was born. He was an only child.

I attended Zenos Coleman Elementary School, which I completed in January 1947. I had a typical childhood of the era. Many young people my age, all African Americans, lived in a largely residential community. We did the usual things and had great fun. Most of the young people with whom I grew up did not attend college. Those of us who did became part of a generation of African Americans in the early 1950s who had different expectations for ourselves than had previous generations, or at least so we thought.

My teachers in elementary school were all Negroes; that was what we called ourselves then. They were excellent teachers, and they were disciplinarians, taking no foolishness from their students. Corporal punishment, while rare, did occur. This usually amounted to a few swipes across the rear end with a yardstick. The teachers and the principal had African American backgrounds. Most of my family attended the same elementary school. My aunts and uncles, and particularly and especially my brother, had a record of doing very well; thus, the teachers had expectations that I, too, would do very well. When I went on to high school I encountered similar expectations.

My family lived on the south side of Chicago, but other members of the extended family lived on both the west and the south side of the city.

Growing up in Chicago, I lived in an all African American community. I had few contacts with anyone my age from the larger white population. Jews owned the local grocery store, but they were also a minority group. African American men owned the local drug store, the candy store, the florist shop, and the dry cleaners. We lived over the grocery store. The nearest white neighborhood was a mile away on the other side of the railroad tracks, to the west. Occasionally, we had some interactions with the white kids, but they always resulted in fights. Whites held all of the jobs on the streetcars that came regularly through our community; we always saw whites on those streetcars. Whenever I went shopping with my mother downtown, we had lots of contact with white Americans as salespersons. As a general matter, I did not experience a great deal of discrimination as a child. Nonetheless, I had a consciousness of white domination.

Whenever groups of us gathered to sit around, we always talked or joked about the white man. We did not understand the full ramifications of our condition, as we were young and in school but not yet well educated. Most of what we received came from our parents or from other elders in the community. I can recall, for example, the Saturday trips to Rufus' Barbershop, where the men talked a great deal. Men of the community gathered there regularly to discuss the condition of African Americans and how whites affected it. Sometimes they grew very frustrated about the whole thing and threw up their hands in disgust. As a child I would just sit and listen. This was an educational experience for me in race relations.

At home I grew up without strong feelings of prejudice against the whites but with a clear understanding that they dominated the African American community. For example, my grandfather and I would regularly watch the Wednesday night fights. Papa never referred to the fighters as either African American or white. He always referred to them by the color of their trunks—the black trunks or the white or light trunks. I find that most interesting as I reflect back on it. My grandfather had very different experiences than I with the larger white community.

Papa, as I called my grandfather, had grown up on a farm in Kentucky. It was a period when blatant discrimination and segregation were rampant in society, and this was true for Kentucky. Nevertheless, he did not talk much about race relations. His father, Bramlett Jones, did not tolerate discrimination and segregation against himself. As an example, when farmers harvested wheat in this part of Kentucky, they would do one farm at a time. Everyone would work a farm until the wheat was in—African Americans and whites together. When they broke for lunch, however, African

Americans had to eat separately from whites. Bramlett Jones would not allow that when they worked his farm. He insisted that at his home they would all eat together or not eat. This was a strange and courageous thing to do in this era. My grandfather ultimately married and migrated with Emma Jones to Springfield, Illinois. There he became first a footman, at the end of horse and carriage days, and then a chauffeur for the attorney general of Illinois. When he moved to Chicago, he worked in the garage of a large high rise on North Lake Shore Drive until his death in 1965.

The children in my neighborhood did all the usual things that children do. In the summers we played all day. Then we went into our homes, cleaned up, changed our clothes, and went out for evening play with the girls. World War II was underway, so we played many war games. We also played softball, football, "not it" (or tag), and hide and seek. We made most of our toys, as our families did not have the money to purchase them. These included "guns" from pieces of wood and parts of inner tubes and scooters from two-by-fours, milk crates, and old roller skates. The girls jumped rope, skipped hopscotch, and roller skated. The boys organized softball teams and football teams around clubs. I can recall my brother, Howard, being a member of the Trojan's Softball Team; I became a junior Trojan. Boy, was I proud of my brother and happy to be a junior Trojan! We regularly played softball. Local businesses would sponsor the teams and provide funds to purchase uniforms for the older boys. Invariably, after these softball games, no matter who won, there were brawls because one team was upset over its loss. The teams lived in different neighborhoods of no more than one or two square blocks. We were quite territorial. We had social functions and athletic functions. I had a great time with the guys while growing up, but I must admit that I never had the reputation of being a strong young man as some did. I did always have the reputation of being intelligent, however, and many of my friends were the tougher guys in the neighborhood, which proved to be a benefit to me. Our social functions were no more than local neighborhood parties with free admission. No one from another region would be welcome. There were the inevitable efforts to crash parties that led to struggles and fights. Guns were rarely used in these fights. I cannot recall anyone being shot.

Some good things came from the clubs or "gangs" that may not seem good to the reader. There was food rationing during World War II, and ration stamps were needed to buy things like butter, eggs, and meat. There were definite shortages of foodstuffs during World War II. On State Street I can recall produce trucks that had stopped at the light at 43rd Street being boarded by local gangs, like the "Four Corners Group." They would break open the tailgates and toss boxes of produce into the street. People from the community would rush out to pick up these boxes, which often contained food and other goods. Groups like the "Four Corners" were feared, but at the same time the neighborhood kids occasionally enjoyed the benefits. An older youth who regularly robbed the local drug store had a large supply of comic books in a shed at the back of his house, where he kept his goods, and he let us younger kids read the comic book collection he had assembled.

I went to church as a child. My parents attended Liberty Baptist Church, and I went to Sunday school there. I did not much enjoy church, although I must admit I did come to love the music, especially the spirituals. I did not like the preoccupation with death and the hereafter. I enjoyed going to the movies on Sunday. I would often skip Sunday school and take my money for the collection plate to use as "show fare." My mother never discovered that. I went with my friends to the movies every Saturday and Sunday afternoon. The movies provided great relaxation, except the cartoons, which typically had negative stereotypes and caricatures of African Americans that we all resented. Occasionally, we saw movies with all African American actors, such as *Cabin in the Sky* and *Stormy Weather*. Other movies with a racial theme, such as *Pinky*, dealt with African Americans passing for white. These experiences also served to create a racial consciousness early in my life. When I grew older I regularly attended the Regal Theater, where over many years I saw and heard virtually every big jazz band in the country. These included Duke Ellington, Louis Jordan, Lionel Hampton, and Billy Eckstine (when he had a band and played a valve trombone). The bands invariably had a stage show with such notables as Dinah Washington, Sarah Vaughan, Pegleg Bates, Al Hibbler (the blind African American singer), and many others. In short, I grew up immersed in the black experience and carried it with me throughout my life.

These were the times of my youth. People like Bonky (Allen) Cooper, the Tyler brothers (Allen, Arthur, and Willie), Alfred White, Willie White, Little Junior, Louis Pickette, William Primous, Thaddeous Nix, Frank Nix, Lillian (Fatso) Murrough, Donna Murrough, Barbara Jean Long, Joyce Roberts, and so many others were my friends. I enjoyed the days of my youth and largely survived them, except one scrimmage in elementary school. A group of my friends and I hit a new boy in the head with rocks. There was no reason for this—just meanness! He was a quiet and unassuming young man, but he had difficulty making friends. One day, lacking anything else to do, we chased George home, not allowing him to enter school that day, by throwing rocks at him. One rock hit George in the head, caused some bleeding, and required some stitches. A fright went through me when he returned to school later that day with his parents and a police officer. They went from class to class, including my class, picking out the young men who were responsible. Of course, we all denied it. No one would admit being there. We had to go to the 48th Street police station to meet with police representatives. When they questioned us, each of us broke down and admitted our involvement but denied hitting him with the rock. As punishment we had to join the Junior Police Force, which met weekly at police headquarters. We accepted it gracefully. A year or two later my elementary school homeroom teacher had any reference to that incident removed from my files. I was so fortunate to have that kind of support and contact in the schools.

As a child I also regularly visited the farm in Kentucky. My grandfather, James L. Jones, always went to Kentucky every summer and had a reunion there with his brothers, John, Forest, and Alex. My grandmother did not like to visit Kentucky, but she did go on one trip in 1938 or 1939. My mother also accompanied us, as did my Aunt Christine and my brother. We took the train from Chicago to Louisville, Kentucky. How I loved the train ride back in those days! I remember counting the telegraph poles as we sped along at what I considered high speeds. The trains and other transportation were segregated, especially in the South, back in that period. We always carried our own food on the train because Indiana and Kentucky practiced discrimination. When we arrived by train in Louisville, we would go to the bus depot and wait for a bus to take us down to Columbia, Kentucky. Once I boldly walked into this big, beautiful restaurant with all the tables set with white cloths, and my mother told me that I had to come back out of that room. I did not understand the reason at the time, but clearly there was a "whites only" rule, and African Americans had to eat in a separate restaurant. This, of course, was why we brought our own food on these trips, so that we were not subjected to such indignities.

Our farm was about five miles outside Columbia. Everyone knew the location of the Jones farm. I can remember in later years when we drove to Columbia we would ask in town about which road to take for the Jones farm. Invariably, the old timers were the ones we asked—they were usually white—and they always knew. The Jones had owned this farm for a long time. On about 150 acres, the family grew corn, wheat, and tobacco and maintained farm animals, including hogs, milk cows, chickens, and horses. I had my first real view of what you might call an "ornery" mule in Kentucky. I think I may have ridden my first horse there, but I did not ride the mule. The mules served as work animals to draw the grass cutter and other farm tools.

We had a cave on the farm from which we drew water for cooking. In that time, the house had no running water. If you wanted a bath, you had to heat water. (We had to do that sometimes at home in Chicago, because the hot water heater ran out regularly, particularly on weekends.) On my first trip to Columbia, my Aunt Christine, my brother, our cousin Palmer, and I went into town to the drug store, sat at the main counter, and had ice cream or ice cream sodas. This was a "no, no" back in the late 1930s and 1940s. The owner put up with our behavior, I understand, because the local whites knew we were with the Jones family, only visiting for the summer, and would soon be gone.

In the late 1930s Uncle John, a brother of my grandfather, somehow managed to mortgage the farm. He used the money to open a restaurant and purchase properties in Logansport, Indiana. He then neglected to pay off the mortgage. Uncle Forest learned of the problem while in Canada, moved to Columbia, and worked off the mortgage. Eventually his son, Willard, joined him. They managed to make a living on the property by growing tobacco, corn, and other crops. Later, Uncle John, the youngest brother of the family, went back to Kentucky from his businesses in Indiana and built a state-of-the-art house on the property. It had inside toilets and hot and cold running water in the kitchen and bathrooms. People came from all around the county to look at Uncle John's house. Uncle Forest always resented Uncle John for doing what he did.

In Chicago during the late 1930s and 1940s, of course, I went to school. In grade school we were very disciplined. Students marched in single file from class to class or in rows of four to six when leaving the building at the end of the day. All classes said the Pledge of Allegiance to the Flag at the start of every class day, and for us it was not "a nation under God." We would raise our hands and point to the flag. During the war years this became too much like the Hitler salute, so the practice stopped.

In preparing for graduation from elementary school and the eighth grade, we composed essays in which we speculated on our future. I wrote that I wanted to be an engineer. Later in the year my essay became the basis for a discussion with my homeroom teacher, my mother, and me. I distinctly recall my teacher asking me what kind of engineer I wanted to become. (We were having a conference to plan the curriculum that I would follow in high school.) When I hesitated in giving my response, she started noting chemical, electrical, civil, mechanical, and so forth. What my teacher never knew was that my ambition at the time was to become a train engineer, but I was even more hesitant to bring it up since my teacher never mentioned this career. Instead, I picked chemical engineer from her list. A Christmas or two earlier I had received a chemistry set as a gift and thoroughly enjoyed playing with it.

As a result of this parent/teacher/student conference I went on to Jean Baptiste Pointe DuSable Senior High School. The staff at DuSable included African Americans and whites, but the students were all African Americans. There I took a college preparatory curriculum in science, mathematics, English, Spanish, and social studies. I often wonder what would have become of me if I had had the nerve to say that I wanted to be a train engineer instead of a chemical engineer!

Graduation from elementary school in Chicago was a big event. We had a formal ceremony in which we wore blue and white ribbons. I often think that we should have more formal ceremonies associated with life's transitions in the early years, as I did during my youth.

I graduated in January 1947 from elementary school and went on to DuSable, where I had four great years. Besides the college preparatory curriculum that I followed, I was active in the Negro History Club, the Pan American Club, the Chemistry Club, the Physics Club, and many others. I also participated in the Junior ROTC Program. DuSable was unique in having an annual formal military ball that all the young ladies wanted to attend. I rose to the rank of captain, and upon graduation from high school I received a brevet commission (signed by Governor Adlai Stevenson) in the Illinois National Guard. I never used the commission.

At DuSable we were the class of January 1951. As young people on the south side of Chicago, we had a great concern with becoming a part of the larger society. This was shown in several ways, one of which I will cite. My high school, named after the first settler in the Chicago area, who happened to be a Frenchman of African descent, was largely African American. Unlike previous graduating classes, we wanted to have our senior luncheon and prom outside the African American community. Our teachers were upset when we told them of our plans, but we moved ahead anyway. We settled for the Hyde Park area, which had a reputation for liberalism, but when we tried to schedule our senior luncheon at a hotel in the area, we found that they were resistant to scheduling anything for African Americans. We persisted, and although we did hold our senior prom at the Parkway Ballroom, we did not hold our senior luncheon there. Instead, it was in Hyde Park at the International Center on the campus of the University of Chicago. This was a significant change, and greater changes were to come in the classes that followed my own.

In 1950—my senior year—no college recruiters came to our high school. Most African American students from the south side during this period went on to either Chicago Teachers College (now Chicago State University) or Wilson Junior College (now Kennedy-King, Jr. College). Our class again wanted to be different.

A few of us sought out a nearly all-white and largely Jewish school on the west side of town, Herzl Community College, in the middle of a transitional community. We took gym classes at the Jewish Community Center. I can recall swimming there. Those of us who attended Herzl were a few African American students in a sea of whites, for the first time in our life. This experience again speaks to our desire to break out of the African American community—from the so-called ghetto—and into the larger society.

As I reflect upon what we view as the civil rights movement of the 1960s, we must acknowledge the rumblings and movements throughout the 1940s and 1950s, and the whole post-World War II era, stemming from African American communities striving to become a greater part of the larger society.

Herzl Community College did not meet my expectations, but I was clearly not ready to commit myself to college at that stage. I eventually left Herzl and took a job in downtown Chicago at the American Fore Insurance Company. There I worked as a clerk delivering mail from one department to another. That job lasted a year before I found another as a meter reader with the Thomas Edison Company. I enjoyed the freedom and flexibility of this job, and through it I learned my way around Chicago for the first time. As a meter reader I saw most neighborhoods. I entered most basements, backyards, bedrooms, and any other places where electric meters were kept. The dogs finally drove me away from that job, and I took a position in Cicero, Illinois, at the Western Electric Company. As a relay adjuster at Western Electric I worked a piecework line for a little over a year before I decided to move on. I made a major change in my life. This I did in fall 1953, much to the dismay of my mother.

▼ ▼ ▼

In 1953 I realized that my life had no direction. I had no savings, although I had purchased a car. I began to wonder seriously what I would do with my life. I decided that it would be best for me to join the military service. Following the outbreak of the Korean conflict I had not joined immediately upon completion of high school, as had a number of my classmates. Many were either wounded or killed in Korea, which could have been avoided, since there was no draft for men seventeen and eighteen years of age. When I decided to join, I searched for a branch that required fewer years of service, but eventually I picked the Marine Corps over the Army, even though it required three years rather than the Army's two. Both my brother and my uncle had served in the Marine Corps.

I went through basic training at the U.S. Marine Corps Recruitment Depot in San Diego, California, beginning September 14, 1953. On September 13 I took my first airline trip, on American Airlines, out of the old Midway Field in Chicago.

The U.S. Marines did not offer a totally new experience for a young African American man from Chicago, particularly one with four years of ROTC and the rank of captain. Much of what they taught in basic training I already knew. For example, I could field strip the M1 rifle blindfolded long before joining the Marines. I also knew close order drill. Many other young men in my platoon struggled with basic training. Most of them were white, although President Truman had integrated the military services shortly after the beginning of the Korean conflict. For me this meant two or three African Americans in a platoon of thirty-five or so men in basic training. Most of the men came from rural Texas, and only a few of us, African American and white, came from urban centers in the Midwest and other parts of the country. One young man who observed me composing a letter home asked me to help him with writing his. He liked the appearance of my letters; the words in his were bunched together in the middle of the page. This gives you an idea of the level of education of some men then in the Marine Corps. This experience confirmed for me the quality of education I had received in Chicago.

I also became interested in chess and began to play daily; I learned to play from some of the men, most of whom were white, and most of whom, like me, came from urban areas in the Midwest. Many of them had plans upon completion of their military service to go back home and go to college. At this time, similar thoughts began to enter my own mind.

Boot camp at Marine Corps Recruit Depot in San Diego was quite an experience. I was one of the three African Americans in our platoon, as I noted earlier. Most of our time was spent learning good discipline and other military things, with which I was already familiar. I learned I would be going to Korea upon completion of my training. We were all encouraged to go to church. While I had never attended church regularly, I had been raised in the Baptist Church and later, along with my grandparents and my mother, had joined the Lutheran Church. I decided to be baptized by a Lutheran chaplain while I was in San Diego.

I became even more motivated to go to college by an experience that took place in infantry training at Camp Pendleton. While out practicing trench warfare in the hills of southern California, I received a call to come back to the base for a physical examination. I learned that my high performance on the General Classification Test (GCT), administered to all those who enter the service, qualified me for consideration as an officer and a pilot in a U.S. Marine Air Wing if I wished, and if I passed the physical. Of course, African Americans were scarce in the Marine Corps, and African American officers or pilots were virtually nonexistent. I did not pass the physical. Nevertheless, this experience changed my life. For the first time, I received independent information that I was highly qualified for further education. College then became an essential feature of my plans following my tour in the Marines. I was denied the opportunity to become an officer and possibly an Air Marine, and I continue to believe this was because the Marines were reluctant to accept an African American into the Officer Corps, let alone as a pilot.

I served in Korea from January 1954 to January 1955. The Korean War had begun in 1950, following the invasion of South Korea by North Korea. The United States entered the war under the auspices of the United Nations, allegedly to protect democracy in South Korea from the Communist regime in North Korea. This conflict was a key event for America in the Cold War, and almost as important on the national scene was the policy of racial integration in the armed forces. President Truman had integrated the services after persistent pressure from many forces, especially civil rights organizations and the outspoken U.S. Representative Adam Clayton Powell.

We traveled to Korea by ship, which took over 22 days. I thought we would stop in Hawaii, but no such luck. We sailed on and on until we reached Sasebo, Japan, and then we moved on to Kobe, where I had my first experience of another culture. They even drove on the wrong side of the road. We arrived in Korea two days later. It resembled a distant, gray, desolate island that grew larger and larger, and more defined, but not more attractive. I wondered at that point, for the first time, if I would see home again.

In Korea I joined with the Fifth Marine Regiment, whose combat history began in World War I and included the Pacific campaigns in World War II. Now it was stationed near the Imjin River and the famous Freedom Bridge in the demilitarized zone. My particular assignment was with the headquarters and supply company of the Second Battalion. My duties were to keep track of various supplies within the company, and I worked under an African American sergeant named Edwards, with whom I shared a tent. Each day we could observe the representatives of neutral forces driving through our area to Panmunjom, where they met in the continuing peace talks that had brought an end to the fighting. There was not much to do in camp. Occasionally, there was some excitement when North Koreans tried to get through our area into South Korea. These "line crossers" came singly rather than in groups. I became aware of the international nature of the armed forces in Korea when one Sunday morning a group of Australians came into our area and offered to trade cases of Asahi beer for some large timbers that we had. We made the trade! I can recall their comment that "we can get all the beer we want, but no bloody timbers."

After three months on the front our regiment moved back to a rear area. The lieutenant in charge of our platoon asked me if I wanted a special assignment. I responded "no." Volunteering was not considered the thing to do, but after talking it over with Sergeant Edwards, I changed my mind. I was sent back to an area called "Charlie Block," where I ran a laundry for the next nine months. A Korean husband and wife team—Chir Gin Sook and Hong Song Hai—actually ran the laundry. They had a daughter whom we called "Skosh Katy." Twenty Korean women washed clothes for the men in my battalion, using the old method of beating the clothing against rocks in the river. After rinsing they hung them out to dry on barbed wire. We provided the soap and paid the women $1.00 a day. This was to be quite an experience for me.

I came to know the Korean family and many of the women very, very well. We developed a close relationship. I lived in a tent at the laundry site. It was my responsibility to handle the money and see to it that no problems arose. Hong Song Hai and his wife actually did all the direct supervision of the women. I learned from them why I had been asked to take up this assignment. The previous person in charge had been an air officer, a Lieutenant Peterson, who happened to be African American. Apparently, they wanted another African American because the lieutenant had gotten along so well with the Koreans. Lieutenant Peterson went on to become an air ace and rose to the rank of lieutenant general. I spoke with him in the late 1980s regarding his experience with the Korean family, and he remembered them.

I thoroughly enjoyed my experiences in Korea. After a year I returned to Southern California with my regiment, the Fifth Marines, the first contingent of the First Marine Division to return to the United States. My remaining 20 months in the Corps were spent in Oceanside, at Camp Pendleton. Nothing major occurred during this time other then the usual racial discrimination. I encountered it in Oceanside shortly after returning from Korea. I was refused service in the local bar, and I reported this to my battalion commander, Lt. Col. Wilson. The bar was put off limits. Col. Wilson was a Congressional Medal of Honor winner who went on to become Commandant of the Marine Corps during President Reagan's administration. I encountered blatant racial discrimination in Amarillo, Texas, while returning home by car with other white Marine buddies. Each of us wore our uniform with Korean service ribbons, but a road stop cafe owner refused us service because I was with them. We drove on in the early morning hours to Oklahoma, where we got service. This was 1955. I was honorably discharged from the Marine Corps in September 1956, following their unsuccessful attempt to get me to "re-up" by offering an assignment in Florida at a Marine air base.

Looking back on that enlistment in the Marines, I fully appreciate the dividends it provided. I had gone in well prepared by having served in my high school's ROTC, and the encouragement to apply for a commission certainly enhanced my self-esteem. For the greater part of those three years I found that the men I served with were fair minded. This was, after all, my first real experience in an organization, in a world for that matter, dominated by whites. I came away proud of my service, self-confident, and competitive. As we used to say in the Marines just after boot camp: "We expect the Navy to step aside!"

After my release from the Marine Corps I returned to Chicago and resumed employment at Western Electric, where I again worked as a relay adjuster. Meanwhile, I registered to attend the University of Illinois.

My mother at this time married a man she had been close to for several years and who was well known and loved by the family. This was Harry Posey, or Scottie, as he was known to all. Scottie was a fine man and stepfather. We had great times together. Long after I was married, we continued to go fishing together on Lake Michigan. When I visited Chicago, I always made it a point to bring my fishing rod.

▼

CHAPTER TWO

UNDERGRADUATE COLLEGE & UNIVERSITY DAYS, & THE WOMAN OF MY LIFE

In January 1957 I became a student at the Navy Pier (Chicago) branch of the University of Illinois. I made use of the Korean G.I. Bill for part of my college education and thereby became the first member of my family to attend a university. I was a "first generation" college student. While attending, I also worked at Western Electric on the evening shift in order to extend my G.I. Bill benefits for as long as possible. Initially, I majored in chemical engineering, but I soon changed to chemistry because of the greater flexibility provided by the curriculum.

I enjoyed the University of Illinois, though in 1957 few African American students attended. At lunch we all sat at one table in the center of the cafeteria. Because most had only recently graduated from high school, and I was 23 years old, we had little in common. I tended to be a loner at the university and associated mainly with the students in my classes.

When I finished the Navy Pier two-year program, I assumed that I would transfer to the main campus at Champaign-Urbana. As it turned out, in summer 1959 I succeeded in getting a job at the Illinois Institute of Technology Research Institute (IITRI) in the Chemical Physics Division. Then called the Armour Research Foundation, it was on 35th and State Street, only 10 blocks from where I had grown up. In all those years I had never known that sometime in the 1940s or early 1950s a nuclear reactor had been located in the Chemical Physics Building at Armour.

At IITRI I worked in radiation chemistry. I was a member of a research group that had a major influence on my attitude and orientation toward chemical research. The group included Paul Feng—from Taiwan—as head. In addition to a number of Americans, there was a Yugoslav and a Czech scientist. As preoccupied as we were with our research, at lunch and during breaks we invariably discussed the events of our time. Of interest to everyone were the developments in Africa, where nations were breaking the shackles of colonialism. Ghana had become independent in 1954. The Congo was going through turmoil in 1959. Lumumba, for example, had declared his country independent, only to be assassinated days later. My experience at IITRI had a major influence on my long-term plans in the field of chemistry. I decided upon completion of my undergraduate studies to pursue a Ph.D. degree.

When I began my work that summer at IITRI, I was planning to transfer to the downstate campus of the University of Illinois, but I was concerned about how I would handle the cost, since the G.I. Bill only provided about $115 per month. I did not have enough money under the bill to cover room and board expenses as well as tuition. I paid only $100 per term tuition at the University of Illinois at Navy Pier. I soon concluded that I wanted to retain my job as a chemical technician at IITRI, where I earned approximately $400 a month—too good to pass up. I looked for an alternate location at which to continue my education and found it in the Evening Division at Northwestern University, located on Chicago Avenue on the near north side. I enrolled there for the next two years, completing my major in chemistry at that institution. I earned a Bachelor's of Philosophy degree in the summer of 1961, the first in my extended family to do so.

At Northwestern University Evening Division I met one professor who had a major effect on my subsequent work—Dr. Fred Basolo, who taught inorganic chemistry. On the first day of class, he passed out a blank Periodic Table and asked everyone in class to fill it out as far as they could. My friend, Ljerka Mamula, had a similar experience and had urged me to learn the Periodic Table before attending Fred Basolo's class. Of course, I filled it out completely. He looked the tables over and asked James Hamilton to stand! That began an excellent relationship that continues to the present. Under Fred Basolo, I earned a master's degree in chemistry on the Evanston campus of Northwestern University.

Northwestern provided a totally new experience for me. There I met, for the first time in my life, middle- and upper-middle-class white Americans, who had all the advantages. Students in some of my chemistry classes went to Aspen regularly for skiing vacations, and I taught them in chemistry laboratories and recitation sections during the two years. There I met largely white American graduate students or African nationals but few African Americans; in chemistry I was the only one. Today, Northwestern leads the Big Ten in the percentage of African American students enrolling.

Fred Basolo had assembled a fine group of young graduate and postdoctoral students. We worked well together. I thought my work at IITRI had prepared me for that kind of experience, and I eagerly took up the challenge of graduate study at Northwestern. I also knew Basolo had an international reputation. Ralph Pearson, professor of physical and inorganic chemistry, also collaborated with Fred Basolo.

The Northwestern of 1961 grew during my stay. I spent many hours sitting on Lake Michigan's shore watching barges come down from the Indiana coast. The barges dumped sand for landfills that would extend the campus into Lake Michigan across the next decade. I met Ruth P. Simms, a Ph.D. candidate in sociology, on that beach front in 1962. We dated for several years and married in 1965.

I had diverse experiences at the Evanston campus. When I arrived, Evanston was a predominantly white suburb of Chicago, with an African American community (living on the west side of town) which had historically worked in a service capacity to the largely upper-class white population. I thought I would have more adjustments to make than I actually did. I had no trouble arranging my accommodations before arriving in Evanston. I lived with a professional chemistry fraternity in Alpha Chi Sigma House, located in an older home on Sherman Avenue, within walking distance of the Technological Institute that housed the Department of Chemistry and several engineering departments. Most of the new graduate students in chemistry lived there. Unfortunately, the Women's Christian Temperance Union had a house nearby. We regularly had problems with that organization after parties, when they discovered empty beer cans on the front lawn.

I moved in with white males from institutions around the Midwest and the nation. They had acquired good undergraduate experiences. The students there, for example, came from DePauw University, Franklin and Marshall University (John Burmeister, now a professor at the University of Delaware, attended this institution), and Wabash College. These small, elite, institutions had a reputation for producing top graduate students in the sciences. This was strong competition for a young African American from inner-city Chicago who had earned his degree in night school at Northwestern. But compete I did.

Study in the department was always challenging. The professors were the best available anywhere in the country. The assignments were always difficult and always interesting. I approached my studies as a loner, which did not serve me well at Northwestern. I learned that many of the students worked on homework assignments together, but I made the discovery too late to help me. Meanwhile, I had become distracted by other matters.

I had discovered the works of W.E.B. DuBois in the library at Northwestern. I began checking out his books and completing the education of an African American male that probably should have begun years earlier in elementary and secondary school. This detracted from my ability to get my work done in a timely manner. By then I had settled upon getting a master's degree by mutual agreement with Fred Basolo. This degree was second prize, not first. But, as I look back upon these early years, I was not ready to devote myself to further graduate work. There was too much else I needed to know—too many cobwebs of the mind that needed clearing away before I could devote myself to a career of study, research, and teaching.

I should note that Northwestern was quite expensive. Because of my planning during my undergraduate years, I still had some of the G.I. Bill left, but every term I had to borrow $500 or more for tuition. This was a sizable sum during that period, but I had had the foresight to establish a good credit rating with a Chicago bank before going to Northwestern. Since I paid my debts on time, I had no difficulty borrowing from the bank.

I mentioned that I met Ruth Simms on the beach front—while sitting on a park bench overlooking Lake Michigan—and that she was working on a Ph.D. in the Department of Sociology. Ruth lived down the street on Sherman Avenue with a number of other women graduate students. My interest in knowing about Africa and African Americans was further encouraged by my developing relationship with Ruth.

It was not uncommon that, walking home from Ruth's house to mine at one or two in the morning, the Evanston police stopped and challenged me under a spotlight to identify myself, with the obvious threat of personal danger if I failed to do so. On one occasion the police stopped me and my Jamaican friend in broad daylight and demanded that we identify ourselves. This occurred within a block of the Technological Institute. When we asked why, the policeman said, and I quote: "A young Black man just snatched somebody's purse."

I had no problems with barbershops in Evanston and had my hair cut regularly at a shop within a block of the Alpha Chi Sigma house, but my experience differed from that of other African Americans and Africans in Evanston. They, along with white students, organized a test of all the barbershops to see which ones discriminated. One shop directly across the street from the Evanston campus was blatantly at fault. My Jamaican friend, Victor Bethune, and two white students made this a test case. One white student was there when my friend entered, and another came later to be present when Victor left the shop. As soon as Victor sat in the barber chair, the barber dramatically closed the blinds. He did cut Victor's hair, but he overcharged him. When Victor left, the white student who remained heard the barbers talk about Victor's unexpected cleanliness and make other racially disparaging remarks. The student tape recorded the conversation, and it became part of the *Northwestern Daily* front-page story on the barbershop issue the next day. The shop was boycotted and picketed by students for weeks afterward.

Of course, racial discrimination was a fact of life all over America. I had not experienced it much because of growing up in a northern city where African Americans lived in segregated ghettos. The civil rights movement had shifted from the South to the North. While I did not directly participate in the movement, like most Americans, including African Americans in northern cities, I observed the events on television, and what I saw deeply moved me. I felt a great sense of pride in the accomplishments of Martin Luther King, Jr., Stokely Carmichael, and many others. Like most African Americans, I also felt anger when I saw them attacked by police dogs, sprayed with fire hoses, beaten with clubs, and battered with rocks and stones by the crowds. I did march once around City Hall in Chicago following a rally in Grant Park at which Dick Gregory spoke. I took a number of pictures at that rally, put them in for developing at a drugstore in Evanston, and never saw them again. To this day I wonder if I was being watched and if my pictures had been confiscated by the FBI. While in Evanston I attended a fund-raising event at a Unitarian church, where the speaker was Rev. Wyatt T. Walker, an advisor to Rev. Martin L. King, Jr. Representatives of the American Legion tried to disrupt the meeting, but the local police ejected them. The activism on campus was good to see and is not evident on campuses today. A greater sense of optimism and better economic conditions prevailed in 1961-63.

I completed my work for the master's degree in chemistry in 1963 and was awarded the degree in 1964. My thesis was "The Substitution Reactions of Bis(ethanolamine)dichloroplatinum (II)." With the assistance of Fred Basolo I made postgraduate plans to take care of personal business, which included getting out of debt by taking a position at Morton Chemical Company. I purchased a car and began working at Morton in fall 1963. Ruth and I had become engaged. I had made a trip to Savannah, Georgia, where I met Ruth's family and friends and came to know Ruth better. While there I met Ruth's father, Wendell, her mother, Ella Ruth, and her brothers, Merilus, Louis, and Richard. (I would later meet her older brother, Robert, who was in the Army.) Richard showed me around Savannah, which like many other southern cities had just ended segregation. Ruth had made frequent visits to Chicago, where she had met my family. Throughout our relationship we were mutually supportive of each other's educational aspirations. I strongly encouraged her to complete her graduate research, which I knew would take her to Ghana for a full year. Meanwhile, I made my plans to stay in Evanston and commute to my job in Woodstock, Illinois, at Morton Chemical Company. Signs on the commuting road called for the impeachment of Chief Justice Earl Warren. Woodstock was John Birch territory, and the conservative movement was growing in the American consciousness. The John Birch Society, a very conservative political organization, had arisen in the late 1950s and early 1960s as a reaction against a perceived liberalism in American society. With that background, I went to Woodstock, and my future spouse went to West Africa.

My mentor and advisor, Fred Basolo, had helped get me the position at Morton, and one of his students, Jay Palmer, became my mentor at the laboratory there. I hope it is now clear how important a mentor can be. Until I went to Northwestern University I had no mentor, although I did have great support from my family and friends. As my mentor, Fred Basolo played a great role in my life. So did Jay Palmer and others.

Woodstock, Illinois, is about 50 miles from Evanston and just beyond the suburban fringe of Chicago. I had purchased a new Ford (1963) upon graduation from Northwestern and began making the commute in fall 1963. From the very beginning I realized that 50 miles one way was a long ride, but I did not want to live in Woodstock, which had a population of 5,000 and no African Americans. Most suburban traffic in the morning went into Chicago, so I put up with the drive.

At Morton Chemical Company I worked with sodium chloride (brines) and magnesium oxide. Morton brought the brines into the laboratory from different parts of Michigan. We precipitated magnesium hydroxide from these brines and made cakes of magnesium oxide, at the time used to coat steel for transformers. Most of it was sold to companies in Germany.

The people at Morton treated me nicely, and I immensely enjoyed working with them. Jay Palmer and his wife, lovely people, invited me into their home on several occasions. Jay realized that I was undecided about my career and encouraged me to go after a Ph.D. He also expressed some regrets that he had settled into an industrial setting.

My commute came to an end in early winter 1963. During a severe snow storm, my car skidded and crashed against a tree. Fortunately, I was not injured, but the car was damaged substantially. I knew immediately that I needed to get some money from the bank and find a place to live in Woodstock. After the accident, I traveled there by train, bought the *Woodstock Times,* and began the search. I will admit that I had reservations and concerns, and I suspected that I would encounter racism in this conservative territory. I saw a notice for an apartment in the home of an elderly woman, called her, and found that it was still available. I took the liberty of telling her in advance that I was African American. If she did not want to rent to me, she could have said so, and thereby saved me some time. To my very great surprise, she had no such reservations. I went out to the house, which was on the same road as the laboratory, liked the apartment and the owner, and rented it right away. This demonstrates that one cannot be guided by one's prejudices and past experiences when dealing with new situations, but must be prepared to deal with the unexpected, and be ready to accept people for what they are rather than what you think they are.

In six months I had my car again, but I continued to live in Woodstock. It was easier than commuting 50 miles.

My work at the laboratory went quite well, but I continued to ponder my future. At one point I considered attending law school and becoming a patent lawyer. Once I thought about getting an M.B.A. With the assistance of my mentors, Basolo and Palmer, I concluded the best thing for me was to go back to graduate school and get my Ph.D.

Fred Basolo wrote on my behalf to Professor Don Martin, at Iowa State University, and to Professor Harris, at the State University of New York at Buffalo. I decided against Buffalo, largely because it was another big city, although not as large as Chicago. I did not see what it could offer me. Ames, Iowa, sounded quite different.

I wanted to see Iowa State, so I arranged to take a trip in spring 1964 with my Jamaican colleague from Northwestern. We took old U.S. 30 directly to Ames, my first automobile trip west of the Mississippi River. We crossed the river into Davenport, Iowa, and from that point on things were different. Iowa was a sea of corn! Corn everywhere. When we arrived at Ames, all I saw was corn. "Where the hell is it?" I said.

Ames, while small, had remained truer to American values of honesty and trust than any city I had been in before. I found that I could cash checks at stores with virtually no identification. If you arrived without a check, the stores had blank checks from every bank in town available for your use. It amazed me that there could be that kind of trust and honesty in America in the 1960s.

My visit to Iowa State was my first substantial contact with a major self-contained university campus. Within the first few days I got oriented to the university and arranged for campus housing in the graduate dorms. I became confident that I would continue graduate study at this institution. I learned later that Antonin Dvorak had visited Iowa State and had written his "New World Symphony" there. The famous African American agronomist George Washington Carver attended ISU and received a master's degree. Finally, Iowa State was a land-grant school. Thus, I was drawn to it because it had historical roots in the African American experience, because it was a school with a specific obligation to the people, and perhaps, too, because Dvorak's great "New World Symphony" pointed me toward my future.

I quickly accepted a graduate fellowship in the Ames Laboratory for summer 1964. This Atomic Energy Commission facility in the middle of the countryside had been constructed and used during the Manhattan Project, which developed the atomic bomb. A good deal of research on metals was being done. The director of the laboratory was Dr. Frank Spedding, who had been part of the Manhattan Project. I recall him as a short, stout, cigar-smoking scientist and bureaucrat who had the respect of his peers.

When I returned to Woodstock, Illinois, I began to make plans for a permanent move to Ames. A most important condition in my life at this time was my continuing engagement to Ruth. She was still in Ghana, and we had made no firm or final plans for our wedding. I wrote her frequently, including some poetry, as I went through all my changes and adjustments. These were difficult times for the country. For example, in 1963, while I was at Morton Chemical and Ruth was in Africa, John F. Kennedy was assassinated. I left work early that day and drove to Chicago in a blinding rain storm to spend the next few days in front of my television, observing tragic but historic events. All the time I wondered what the effect must be on Ruth, to be out of the country when the president was assassinated. I wrote to her about the events. I also explained my plans to resume graduate school at Ames. She was happy to know I was going back to the university, but I am sure she was wondering, "What is this place called Ames?"

▼

CHAPTER THREE

AFRICAN AMERICAN PH.D. PRODUCTION AT IOWA STATE UNIVERSITY

Since Ruth was still in Ghana, I settled into Ames on my own. I had the encouragement and support of my family, but since I was a first-generation college student, my mother, aunts, uncles, and cousins did not understand the transition I was about to make by returning to school.

I traveled to Iowa by way of Kentucky, taking this opportunity to visit with Great-Uncle Forest and Great-Uncle John, who were living on the old family farm. What prompted me to make that large side trip I really do not know. I suspect that it was based upon a deeply instilled respect for my elders that I had acquired as a child, and a deep respect for what they could share with me at this important juncture of my life. No doubt I also just wanted to see the farm in Kentucky and my great-uncles. I had always loved visiting there. So off to Kentucky I went, and I spent three lovely days visiting with these grand old men. Great-Uncle Forest was my grandfather's oldest brother, and Great-Uncle John was a younger brother. As mentioned earlier, Great-Uncle John had left the farm early in life, branched out on his own, and become a successful businessman in Logansport, Indiana. He had done this at the expense of the farm, which he had mortgaged to fund his business ventures, and he had neglected to take care of the mortgage. Taking care of it fell to Great-Uncle Forest, and this had put a permanent distance between them. Great-Uncle Forest would not speak to Great-Uncle John.

During my visit we went to the old church in the area, where I had a chance, for the first time that I could remember, to see the old graveyard and headstones. There I saw the burial site of Bramlett Jones, after whom I named my son. I stayed with Great-Uncle Forest and managed to talk every day to each brother, but never to both at the same time. Great-Uncle John had built his home about 200 yards from the old house and lived there with a woman who for all practical purposes was his wife. Great-Uncle Forest lived in the family home alone. His son, Willard, had died some years earlier. I still carry a vision of Great-Uncle Forest sitting on the back porch in an old chair with his old hat, in bib overalls, puffing on a pipe or chewing tobacco through a white stubbly beard. I would never see either Great-Uncle Forest or Great-Uncle John living again.

From the farm in Kentucky I drove west to Iowa, stopping once at Mammoth Cave for a quick tour. We had a cave on the farm, and I wanted to draw a few comparisons. From there I drove into western Kentucky, where I encountered blatant racial discrimination in motels outside Paducah. Consistently, the clerks would not rent to me "because they were full." I spent the night at a Holiday Inn in town after fruitless hours of search. I left the next day and drove to Springfield, Illinois, my mother's birthplace, and visited with relatives from my grandmother's side of the family, the Nelsons. I stayed with my second cousin, Shirley Barger. She and her husband had a nice home and were willing to put me up. I had a great visit in Springfield and received more support and encouragement. This need to touch base with kin was, no doubt, a consequence of growing up with a relatively large extended family.

After arriving in Ames, I settled into my apartment in the graduate dormitory and into my laboratory in the Department of Chemistry. Professor James Espenson had been assigned as my interim faculty advisor. As I understood it, I was free to make my final choice. My initial assignment to Espenson was based upon his interest in kinetics and my earlier work in kinetic mechanisms with Fred Basolo.

It was summer 1964, and my great concern was to earn my Ph.D. Qualifying examinations in four fields of chemistry—inorganic, analytical, physical, and organic—awaited me, and I intended to spend my summer preparing for them. James Espenson, a dynamic young professor trying to make a mark, wanted me to spend my time that summer doing research. I intended to pass all qualifying examinations, and I applied myself to this task. I put greatest emphasis on physical chemistry and organic chemistry, my weaker areas.

I purchased copies of the two standard texts, Morrison and Boyd's *Organic Chemistry* and Moore's *Physical Chemistry*. I had managed to get a copy of the latter with an answer book for the problems in the back of each chapter. It took me the entire summer to complete them, but I worked every problem in each of these texts, and I mean every problem. When we took the qualifying examinations, I passed all four. I had anticipated no problems with inorganic—the area in which I planned to study. In the final analysis I earned a high pass in two areas and a pass in a third, and I qualified in the fourth area. I was extremely pleased. Dr. Espenson was pleased as well, but by now I felt that our relationship was not a sustainable one, and I began looking for an alternate faculty advisor.

In doing this, I first met with the head of the department, Dr. Charles Goetz, and told him that I wanted to make a change. I received his encouragement and support. That was that! I remember Dr. Goetz well, addressing the new graduate students, and advising us that "if we have emotional, psychological or other problems Iowa State University is surrounded by numerous churches and synagogues filled with individuals willing to be helpful!" Perhaps not so ironically, Dr. Goetz helped me with my problem.

I finally sought out Dr. Robert E. McCarley as my faculty advisor. The research underway in his group on metal-to-metal bonds in discrete molecules and ions attracted me. This I found fascinating and new, so I began working with him later in 1964. My decision to find another advisor had prompted one faculty member to stop me in the hall and point out to me that if I "did not make it with McCarley, I would be through in that department." Those were harsh words but probably reflected reality. I would be successful in earning my Ph.D. under the direction of Dr. McCarley, a quiet, intellectual, detailed, and thoroughly thoughtful mentor. I respected him immensely. His research group was working on the chemistry of early second- and third-row transition elements, such as niobium, tantalum, molybdenum, and tungsten. With one exception, Leda Mueller, the team was all male. Women pursuing Ph.D.s in chemistry were few. I was the only African American in the group. Most of the men were from west of the Mississippi River. We were a very good supportive group and enjoyed one another. We thrived on the research.

I spent the first year in McCarley's group getting to know the nature of the work and the equipment, such as the electron paramagnetic resonance machine and the far infrared spectrophotometer. We did most of our work under inert atmosphere conditions, that is, in the absence of air or oxygen and moisture; the materials would have reacted instantaneously with these substances. Thus, I had to learn how to use an inert atmosphere box, a container of dry nitrogen into which one thrust his hands wrapped in rubber gloves. We also worked with high vacuum techniques, which were familiar to me from my days at IITRI in Chicago. Of course, I also had to get to know the members of the group as well. Most of all, I had to understand the expectations of my major professor.

The year went fairly rapidly, and I enjoyed not only my work within the department but also my classes. Physical chemistry continued to be the most challenging area for me, but I managed an average grade of B.

I also experienced a mild form of racist behavior during my first year at Ames. I went with Clifford Smith, another graduate student, to a concert by Van Cliburn. During intermission an elderly white gentleman approached us and asked how we "boys" were enjoying the concert. While his reference to us as "boys" obviously upset us, we did not directly confront him in the crowded foyer. Instead, I commented to him that I thought this concert, which was being held in a high school auditorium (at this time the university did not have a performing arts center), was reasonably good, but the poor acoustics did not approach the caliber I had expected after seeing Van Cliburn perform at Orchestra Hall in Chicago. The gentleman made no comment and sought excuses for not continuing "a conversation among gentlemen" that he never wanted to have in the first place. Ames was not free of the vestiges of poor race relations, either, but, by and large, the people of Ames were quite friendly, and I came to like this small town where I would spend three more years.

▼   ▼   ▼

Ruth returned from Africa to Evanston to complete her Ph.D. in sociology, and we made plans to be married in July 1965. Two months beforehand, unfortunately, Ruth lost her father, and my grandfather would pass on July 5, 1965. Nevertheless, it was a happy occasion that brought our families together in Savannah, Georgia, on July 3, 1965, where we took the vows of marriage in an old Congregational church in the African American community. My brother, Howard, served as best man.

Ruth's mother and brothers made me feel welcome in Savannah whenever I came, and especially so for the wedding. There could not have been anything more beautiful than our wedding. Ruth was absolutely lovely in her bridal gown. I shall never forget the sight of her coming down the aisle, my relief after the wedding, the lovely reception, our first night together in Savannah, and our flight the next day to Niagara Falls, New York. Niagara Falls would have been better if I had not made our reservations on the American side but on the Canadian side, which had the best view of the falls. But for two honeymooners it did not matter what side we were on—just being there together was everything.

Ruth and I picked up my car in Chicago and drove across country to Ames. We took up residence for the next four years at 2327 Knapp Street, where I rented an apartment within two blocks of the campus Union. It was summer 1965, and I had completed one year of graduate work at Iowa State University.

Ruth had an outstanding background in sociology from Northwestern and experienced no difficulty whatsoever in getting a tenure track assistant professorship in the Department of Sociology and Anthropology at ISU. As a result of her contacts and mine, our network of social and professional relationships significantly expanded. We came to know not only chemists and physical scientists but also others in the social and behavioral sciences.

One couple with whom we developed a very close relationship stands out as quite important to us—Russell Pounds and his wife, Gloria. Russell, a professor in agriculture and extension education, had been at Iowa State some years before our arrival. Both he and his wife were quite active in local and national politics of the day.

David and Hannah Gradwohl also became our friends. David, an anthropologist with whom Ruth shared an office, did excavation and archaeological work in association with the emerging Sailor Dam Project, near the Ledges State Park on the Des Moines River. We came to know David and Hannah very well and spent many rewarding hours in their home. Much could be said as well about Gil and Ann Bartell. Gil, also an anthropologist, impressed me as an unusual individual, quite out of the ordinary, and not the typical professor or scholar. He did research on the Yaqui Indians in southern Texas and Mexico. Gil had learned the chants and dances of this group, and it was not unusual at his lectures for him to appear in full Yaqui dress and do the ritualistic dances with the associated chants and songs.

Ruth and I met a number of African American graduate students from the Department of Chemistry. One who comes to mind was Robert Harrell, a graduate of Morgan State College in Baltimore. Most of the others had also earned their undergraduate degrees in chemistry in historically black colleges and universities (HBCUs). Within several years, five would earn their Ph.D. in chemistry at Iowa State. After graduation, Clifford Smith joined the faculty at an HBCU in Georgia, and Costello Brown went to California State University-Los Angeles. Another joined AT&T Bell Laboratories to become the head of one of their analytical divisions. Thus, there was real talent in this group. I learned a great deal about the HBCUs and the advantages of pursuing an undergraduate degree in such schools. Of course, my wife had earned her undergraduate degree at Talladega College.

The ISU Department of Chemistry's connections with HBCUs had to be related, in part, to Professor Henry Gilman, an organometallic chemist of international stature. He served on the

Board of Trustees of Tuskegee Institute and was well known among those who had connections with HBCUs. Through his efforts and connections Iowa State found itself in the enviable position from 1964-68 of having produced six or seven African Americans with Ph.D. degrees in chemistry.

Gil Bartell, referred to already as an unusual individual, was quite talented and adept with tools. He also had a large sailboat there in the middle of Iowa, which he sailed on Little Wall Lake. For some reason, inexplicable to all except him and perhaps his wife, Gil befriended Ruth and me. We spent many hours in each other's homes enjoying delightful meals and wonderful conversation. Invariably David Gradwohl and others joined us on these delightful occasions at the Bartell's home, sitting around a low circular table in deck chairs. Gil took me sailing, and I was smitten with it immediately. Not long after that he approached me with the unusual idea of constructing our own sailboat from a kit. We went in together and purchased a kit for a Penguin Cat Rigged (single-sail) boat, which we spent most of the winter of 1966 constructing. We gave it its maiden voyage in spring 1966 on Little Wall Lake, quite an adventure, particularly when you realize that neither I nor my wife could swim. We wore our life jackets at all times. Gil, who seemed to have an inexhaustible supply of money, moved up to a Flying Dutchman, a trapeze boat equipped with a spinnaker sail, and we sailed that with him as well. Sailing was also the interest of several members of the faculty in chemistry, particularly Hugh Franzen and Bernard Gerstein. Each had his own sailboat, and we raced them on Little Wall Lake. This background gives a further perspective on the kind of environment available at Ames, Iowa.

I have already noted that Ames was an unusual and different place. "Town and gown" were in part separated by the main street, Lincoln Way, and by vacant farmland on the west side of town. Ruth and I moved to our second residence in "town" in 1966, a duplex at 1317 Harding. It was owned by a graduate student in agricultural economics who seemed to be economically comfortable and whose parents seemed well off. He lived in half the duplex, and we lived in the other. We resided there for the remainder of our time in Ames.

▼   ▼   ▼

In my research at ISU, unlike the research at Northwestern, I made new compounds (synthesis) and defined these compounds by their properties (or characterized them). Bob McCarley's group worked on cluster compounds in which as many as six metals bonded one to the other at the vertices of an octahedron, and these six metals could in turn be bonded to 12 to 18 other chloride ions. The solutions that these formed in alcohol were quite richly colored and a glory to behold. I would subsequently learn that, in fact, early work on these compounds had been done by Linus Pauling, who had done a molecular structure determination of Nb_6Cl_{14} in concentrated alcohol solution. This was fascinating. In my studies of chemical compounds I had not encountered species such as these. They also possessed a high degree of symmetry, and they were susceptible to study by various physicochemical techniques. I began my work looking for compounds of niobium that were of intermediate composition between $NbCl_{2.33}$ and $NbCl_3$.

In my early work in this area I experienced the usual problems of a researcher who sets out to find a particular phenomenon and is frustrated. I must admit that over the first year of my research, some of my fellow graduate students were mildly amused by my efforts. They were seasoned veterans in all the techniques, and I was just learning them. They were willing to help, and I did get assistance from several of them, but only after I overcame my own barrier to seeking such assistance. This is a problem that I had throughout my youth, and as I have grown older I have observed younger people committing the same error. I mean by that the tendency "to make it on your own" and resist seeking the help of others who have traveled down the same path that you are moving on. It is difficult to account for this reluctance. I believe it is probably related to a fear of failure or, more specifically, to the fear of letting anyone else observe me making mistakes and possibly failing. I am very happy to say that I got over it at a relatively young age. I have since found that my progress has been more rapid when I have been able to overcome these barriers to seeking advice and counsel than when I did not.

My ultimate research project, I soon realized, would have to be something that I selected. Everyone was working on the hexanuclear niobium, tantalum, and tungsten compounds. I needed to find something different. I finally began working with dialkylsulfide complexes of niobium(IV). These compounds had the unusual property of adding to metal tetrahalides. But no one had prepared the dialkylsulfide complexes of niobium(IV), so I set out to prepare a series of these compounds: bis(dimethylsulfide)tetrachloroniobium(IV), bis(diethylsulfide)tetrahaloniobium(IV) (halo = Cl, Br, and I), and bis(tetrahydrothiophene) tetrahaloniobium(IV) (halo = Cl, Br, and I). They were very smelly, and I soon developed a reputation in the laboratory for carrying about with me a constant odor of them, but I brushed it off and continued with my research. Needless to say, the preparation of these compounds and the study of their physical properties became the basis for my Ph.D. dissertation research under Bob McCarley. We published three papers together, one on my earlier work with the hexanuclear species and two additional papers on the dialkylsulfide complexes. We discovered some evidence for metal-metal bonding in the sulfides as well when only one alkylsulfide appeared to add to the niobium tetrahalides.

I completed my research in 1968. After presenting a paper on my work to the faculty and to other chemists at the American Chemical Society meetings in San Francisco, I was awarded my Ph.D. that summer.

▼   ▼   ▼

In 1967 Ruth and I were expecting our first child. She was pregnant at the time we took an excursion West. After being in Iowa for only a short time, we soon discovered that most people who lived there did not go East for vacations. On the contrary, they looked to the western states, and we did as well. We had heard a great deal about Grand Teton and Yellowstone national parks from mutual friends, so in summer 1967 we took our camping gear and began a trek West. We had purchased our own camping gear and had gone on several camping trips around Iowa. Our trip was a totally new experience. We went across Iowa and Nebraska and on into South Dakota, camping all along the way. We were naive enough to plan on sailing on Jackson Lake, and we packed our camping gear into our sailboat. We crossed the Missouri River, visited the Badlands of South Dakota, and went to the Black Hills, stopping to see the faces of the presidents at Mount Rushmore. We drove into the Bighorn Mountain Range, down through Shoshone Pass, into Wyoming, and up to the entrance of Yellowstone National Park. It was here that I discovered my fear of heights. I overcame it to do my share of driving in the mountains, but I must admit Ruth took to mountain driving.

We camped in tents in Yellowstone and went about seeing all of the sights in that magnificent park. The bears were begging at cars as we entered the park on that first morning. As we sat in line waiting to get in, we thought how great it would be when we were older to bring our children here on this same kind of trek. We thoroughly enjoyed Yellowstone and then moved on south to visit Grand Teton National Park. The view of the Teton Mountain Range as you enter from the north is purely spectacular. We fell in love with the park immediately. I foolishly put our 11-foot-long sailboat on Jackson Lake and attracted all the kids in the area when our sail went up. We had to leave the lake to the big tour boats, however, as they washed us ashore with their wake. I made only one error in arranging the trip to the Tetons. I intended to spend our first few days in the Grand Teton Lodge in an outlying cabin and the last three days camping. That was not ideal. I believe Ruth would have enjoyed it if we had done that in the reverse. Nonetheless, we had a great time in the Tetons. We saw many, many more animals in the Tetons than in Yellowstone, including elk, moose, antelope, bear, crows, eagles, and many other different species. They paid little heed to us, allowing us to get much closer than one might expect an animal in the wild would allow. We took magnificent photographs and made clear to ourselves that one day we would return to the Tetons.

We also visited Jenny Lake Lodge one afternoon and signed up for one of their special buffet luncheons. You have to appreciate that Jenny Lake Lodge was a relatively exclusive place back in those days. It provided a magnificent view of the Teton Range. I can recall the hostess greeting us when we came to sign up for the luncheon. She told us the cost was $100 per person and that we certainly could sign up, which we did. As a graduate student, I did not have $100 to devote to a dinner at that time, but I was not about to be embarrassed by lack of funds, so I signed up. You can bet that when we got back to our room at the Grand Teton Lodge we enjoyed a big laugh and a great meal! I called and canceled that buffet luncheon. Instead, we spent the money on a float trip on the Snake River and a breakfast ride on horseback. While we were in the Teton area, we also spent time in Jackson Hole and enjoyed a magnificent western musical at one of the local theaters. I began a collection of minerals that I still maintain.

When we returned to Ames, clearly the biggest event to come was the birth of our first child. Ruth's obstetrician, Dr. Dorne, had a clinic across the street from Mary Greeley Hospital in Ames. As the time approached I became more and more nervous, and I am sure that Ruth was concerned even more than I. I recall clearly the day that I took Ruth to the hospital. This was to be an induced labor, in part because of the size of the baby. Ruth and I had been large children at birth, approaching ten pounds each. We arrived at the hospital between 6:00 and 7:00 A.M., as arranged, and shortly thereafter the doctor began inducing labor. I was with Ruth virtually the entire day. One other woman was there, the wife of a faculty member in the Department of Chemistry. She was having some difficulty and at one point screamed rather loudly. This unnerved me but did not seem to have any effect on Ruth, who was quite calm throughout the process. Between 6:00 and 7:00 P.M. Ruth gave birth to our son, whom we named Bramlett Wendell Hamilton. The Bramlett was taken from his great-great-grandfather in Kentucky, and the Wendell came from Ruth's father. Bramlett was born on November 28, 1968, more than nine pounds at birth and a lovely baby. I remember seeing him and Ruth shortly after they came out of the delivery room. He had a full head of hair, and Ruth was in very good shape, smiling and holding our son. Bramlett, of course, would forever change our lives. In fact, he prompted Ruth's mother, Ella Ruth, to leave Georgia for the first time. In January 1969, on an extended train trip through Chicago and cross-country to Ames, she came to visit Ruth and me, and more particularly Bramlett. My mother also visited from Chicago.

▼

CHAPTER FOUR

EXPERIENCES AT MICHIGAN STATE UNIVERSITY & WITH THE MID-AMERICA ASSOCIATION: 1968-1975

I came to Michigan State University after a search among institutions in which to do a postdoctoral research associateship. My application to MSU was prompted by the research of Professor Carl Brubaker in the Department of Chemistry, who had an interest in preparing organometallic compounds of niobium. I was accepted by Dr. Brubaker. In spring 1968 my family, which now included my year-old son, Bramlett, made plans to move to Michigan. Ruth had secured an appointment as a visiting professor in the Department of Sociology.

I knew Michigan State University was a good place to do research in chemistry. Moreover, in a *National Land-Grant Association Newsletter* I had read about the Center for Racial and Ethnic Affairs, proposed by the Committee of Sixteen appointed by MSU President John Hannah. Ron Lee, a White House Fellow, became the first director of that center, renamed the Center for Urban Affairs. Robert Green, a professor of education, would become the second director following Ron Lee's departure to Washington, D.C., to become Assistant Postmaster General. MSU's commitments to African Americans in higher education in the state of Michigan were impressive. This was particularly important to me as an African American, but also because I was leaving a traumatic year of race relations at Iowa State University.

There had been major campus demonstrations at ISU by the larger student body on issues stemming from the Vietnam War, and the African American students there were concerned about the extent of the institutional commitment to their needs. Their activities resulted in the historic "Black Saturday," during which several public forums were held by African American students across the university community for both "town and gown." I spoke at one of these.

My own major professor, Dr. Robert E. McCarley, took an active interest in these developments, which pleased me considerably. His support further catalyzed my greater involvement. The goal of Black Saturday was multiple, including the education of the larger community to African American student concerns and the development of a new consciousness among the African American students themselves, who at this time were making the transition from being called a Negro community to being called a Black community. At the forum in which I participated, a local white resident asked why the students could not continue being Negroes rather than Blacks; he could not see the reason for a name change. A student responded: "That is exactly why we want to change the name. We want to force you to rethink the implications of being a 'Negro' in America." This message is applicable to developments in the late 1980s that led to the shift from a Black community to an African American community.

Our move that spring from Iowa State to MSU occurred at the same time as the assassination of Martin Luther King, Jr. I was at the American Chemical Society meeting in San Francisco to present the results of my dissertation research; it was the morning after his assassination that I had to make my presentation. What a time to be making a transition from Ames, Iowa, to East Lansing, Michigan.

▼   ▼   ▼

Ruth and I drove to Michigan in June 1968 and took an apartment in a duplex at 941 Ann Street, within easy walking distance of the campus. Our new neighbors were a retired couple, the Proctors, who were a delight.

When we arrived on campus, we were not at all surprised by the thousands of people there, but we were struck by the obvious presence of police carrying guns. This had been a rare sight at Iowa State. In fact, when we arrived at MSU, the SDS (Students for a Democratic Society) was holding its annual meeting in Michigan. We were not shocked, but this did surprise us.

The Department of Chemistry was a welcome sight. Jack Kinsinger was the chair, and he greeted me warmly, as did Carl Brubaker, with whom I would be working for the year. The department possessed excellent research equipment and had substantial expertise in electron spin resonance, which I would use in my research. There was one other African American student who had finished his Ph.D. in organic chemistry, Dr. Ron Goldsberry. Because Ruth had quite a different background than I did, I had always enjoyed a much broader range of associates than one might expect for a chemist. It was not long before we established new friends in the East Lansing community, a multiracial and multidisciplinary group that also included many Africans. My wife became a faculty member in the Department of Sociology and was associated with the large African Studies Center at MSU.

As a young African American family we were a curiosity but also of substantial interest to many African American students. This was doubly the case since we both had Ph.D.s—a rarity. Our home became a regular haven for many undergraduate and graduate African American and African students at Michigan State. Our friends, among others, were Richard Thomas, now a professor of history but at the time an undergraduate; June Thomas, then June Manning, an undergraduate who became a professor in urban planning and geography; Barry Amis, then a graduate student in romance languages; Ron Bailey, a very bright undergraduate in political science; John Nabila, a Ghanaian and a Ph.D. candidate in geography under Professor John Hunter; and Alfred Opubor, professor of communications, who would serve a period as director of the African Studies Center and whose home was Nigeria. There were others, including Dozier Thornton, professor of psychology; Irvin Vance, professor of mathematics; the late Leslie B. Rout, professor of history; the late William Pipes, a professor in the

Department of Romance Languages; the late Anna Marie Hayes, a graduate student; and Kamuyu Wakengethe, a graduate student, and his peer, Mina, both from Kenya.

▼   ▼   ▼

During my postdoctoral year in the Department of Chemistry I had a range of different and unique experiences that transcended chemistry and involved me in broader university affairs in a way I had not anticipated but which did not surprise me. As early as the fall term, I was approached by African American students who sought my assistance with problems they were having in first-year chemistry courses. This was part of a much larger issue, as I was to learn about from Dr. Robert L. Green, director of the Center for Urban Affairs, who in 1969 called a meeting of African American faculty and graduate students to discuss the problem. So when I was approached by African American undergraduates in chemistry I responded by providing them with direct assistance. But soon their numbers grew to the point where it became too much for me to do and complete my work in Carl Brubaker's group. I then took a unique step.

The Center for Urban Affairs had been created with a budget of $1.5 million. These funds were used to expand educational opportunities for African American and other minority students, faculty, and other professionals at Michigan State University. The Center for Urban Affairs was created in controversy, as many deans of colleges within the university felt that the funding for Urban Affairs had been at their expense. This concern would plague the center throughout its existence and would be amplified later, when the center developed new enemies in the legislature. I was aware of these funds as early as 1968 from my associations with Robert Green and others. I wrote a proposal to the center in 1969 requesting funds to help African American students in chemistry.

This project, which I called Project TAC (Tutorial Assistance in Chemistry), was funded by the EOP (Educational Opportunity Program) in 1969. We began in the fall of that year to offer a formal program of tutoring to African American engineering majors. I was the first person to manage the program. If I had had the foresight, I would have insisted that the funds for graduate assistants in TAC be assigned to African Americans. In this way we could have increased the number of African Americans recruited for graduate study in chemistry, but, alas, my interest and focus were on African American undergraduates. The graduate students that I selected included some very talented individuals, such as a National Science Foundation Fellow named Dale Work. Project TAC has continued as one of the Department of Chemistry's major efforts to improve the study of chemistry by African Americans. The students admitted to Project TAC largely had been underprepared in high school. I set criteria of a 2.4-2.75 GPA from high school and a minimum SAT of 800. This seemed to work very well. Later, these same criteria would be adopted by the university for the Detroit Project and its successors. In spring 1993, Project TAC (now called the Drew TAC Program) received the annual MSU Diversity Award.

Through Project TAC I met many young African American students in engineering, since most of the African American science students were not majors in chemistry. They were members of an organization called Black Students in Engineering. That college, like many others across the country in those early years, had become actively involved in the recruitment and academic support of African Americans. In 1970, my assistant, Barbara Gunnings, pointed out an African American student from Detroit who rejected being taught or tutored by white students. I had a long discussion with Larry Walker. Years later, Larry earned a bachelor's degree in physics (not known for having many African Americans) and later a master's degree and Ph.D. in agricultural engineering (also not known for having many African Americans). He is now professor of biological sciences and agricultural engineering at Cornell University. Gregory Reed, another African American I met through this program, majored in packaging. When we talked, he was planning a trip to Spain as part of the MSU Overseas Program. He is now a successful lawyer and financial planner in the greater Detroit area. A third man, George Simmons, quite exceptional in his background, was never known to earn anything less than a 4.0.

George completed a bachelor's in electrical engineering at MSU, was immediately hired by Bell Laboratories, and was sent by them to the University of Michigan in Ann Arbor to study for the master's degree. He then went to work for Bell Laboratories in New Hampshire and later moved to the facilities in Naperville, Illinois. He ultimately earned his Ph.D. in two years in electrical engineering at Michigan State. Simmons now has a lovely family and has moved to the Carolinas, where he is vice president for sales and marketing in a subsidiary of Bell Laboratories.

These African Americans were students coming out of Detroit, which in 1967—during their last years in high school—experienced major racial turmoil and riots. They had very negative attitudes toward the larger society as they entered Michigan State University. Most went on to achieve great things at and beyond the university. Their experiences are typical of the African American students who entered MSU in the late 1960s and early 1970s.

During my postdoctoral year at Michigan State I actively sought a faculty position in a department of chemistry. I received an offer from Southern University at Baton Rouge, among others, during an extended trip that I made for the MSU Department of Chemistry to recruit African American graduate students. That trip was my first major exposure to HBCUs. I began my trip in Maryland with a visit to Morgan State University and continued into the Carolinas and Georgia, visiting North Carolina Central University, South Carolina State University, Savannah State University, and the Atlanta University Complex (including the campuses of Morehouse, Spelman, and then Clark University). I went from there to Florida A&M University and Southern University at Baton Rouge and at New Orleans, Louisiana. At each stop I presented a seminar on metal-metal bonding in dialkylsulfide complexes of niobium(IV) and related metal-metal bonded complexes of niobium and tantalum. There was great interest in my research everywhere I went, and much to my surprise there was interest in me. While, on the one hand, I went about recruiting students for MSU, on the other hand, everywhere I went I was recruited to join the faculty. At South Carolina State University the president said he would create a chemistry division and make me the head of it. This was not an atypical response of institutional representatives. I was surprised to find that even as late as 1968 and 1969 many faculty on these campuses were not African American. On the contrary, many were of East Indian descent or were from the Middle East. There were a few who were white. At Lincoln University in Pennsylvania, the first HBCU in the United States, the Department of Chemistry was headed by a white professor, DeForrest Rudd, who had earned his Ph.D. at Harvard University. He had built an excellent small department with strength in spectroscopy.

During this period, Michigan State University was under significant pressure to increase the number of African American faculty. I learned of a vacancy in the Department of Chemistry, immediately applied for the position, and was hired. Although the starting salary was below that offered by Southern University, MSU also proposed $10,000 in research allowance. The chairperson at the time was Jack Kinsinger. The inorganic chemistry faculty included Carl Brubaker, Harry Eick, Tom Pinnavaia, Bob Hammer (Honors College), Kim Cohn, and C. McCarty (General Chemistry).

My graduate students in chemistry came because of the kind of research in which I was engaged, and I also think because I was the only African American professor in the Department of Chemistry. In fact, I believe I was the first African American professor to join the department. My first graduate student, Kirby Kirksey, was about my height (six feet), a very dark African American, and a great hulk of a man. He was quite eloquent in his speech and a very nice person. Kirby began working with me on complexes of niobium tetrahalides with dimethylformamide. He earned his master's degree based upon the work he did on the formamide complexes of niobium. He went on to do Ph.D. work on "ESR Studies of 1, 1 Dithiol Complexes with Niobium(IV)." Kirby came to me from Texas Southern University, and I had thought that when he finished he might return there, take up a faculty position, and teach; but Kirby had other plans.

My second student, Roger N. McGinnis, was white, and he and his spouse, Eva, were from Michigan. Roger was quite sharp and had done his undergraduate work at MSU. It was unusual for him to be seeking a Ph.D. at the same institution, but nonetheless he did. Roger undertook research on diethyldithiophosphate complexes of niobium(IV).

My third student was Bobby Lee Wilson, from Mississippi, who had a bachelor's degree from Alabama A&M University. Bobby was an African American, somewhat older, with a family. He initially studied dialykldithiocarbamate complexes of niobium(IV) but later shifted his focus.

All three of these students overlapped in my research group. They were assigned teaching duties in the department and undertook research for the remainder of their time. I had received a petroleum research fund grant that helped to pay for some of their research time in the summer. In addition, I had obtained support for a graduate student from the Center for Urban Affairs and EOP programs as early as 1970. Kirby Kirksey received these funds.

During this time, I also taught chemistry courses at the undergraduate level as well as a special topics course and seminar at the graduate level. The general reception to me by students and other faculty was always positive, but also always curious. There inevitably were instances in which white students would see me after class and challenge my knowledge of the subject matter. I know that for most students in the first-year chemistry classes I was the only African American teacher with whom they ever had contact, but this never presented any major problems. In one course that I taught one year, Chemistry 142, I did experience a minor problem. This course had a reputation for attracting pre-medical students with interest only in the highest grades they could get. I learned through a student in the course that some white students were concerned that I was not as knowledgeable as I might be of the subject matter. I was also informed that they were cheating, although I could never prove this. I did learn that some students' concerns were grades that were not as high as they had planned to receive. For the rest of my career at MSU I taught first-year students in general chemistry and chemistry majors (seniors) an advanced inorganic course.

I was also assigned advisees after I joined the department. Among them was a young African American woman named Daralyn Waters, a chemistry major, who was from Baltimore,

Maryland. I met with Daralyn often, but at the end of her first term at MSU she did not return. She had not had an outstanding term, but neither had she failed. The assistant dean, John Zimmer, suggested that I telephone her and try to get her back. I did that, Daralyn returned, and she subsequently earned her degree in medical technology.

My administrative work, about which I say more later, began in 1971, at the time that I was launching my research with the graduate students. This was asking much of me by central administration, and I was asking much of myself. As I reflect back upon it, although all my students earned their Ph.D. degrees, I believe they did not benefit at all from my assumption of responsibilities in 1971 as assistant provost for special programs. In fact, I moved out of the chemistry building into offices in central administration and spent less and less time in chemistry. I also did not publish as many papers on my work. My attention had been divided between administration and research. I note with pleasure that each student earned his Ph.D. degree. Roger was first, then Kirby Kirksey, then Bobby Lee Wilson. Their dissertations were approved by their committees, and they graduated and went to other duties and responsibilities.

Kirby Kirksey had been recruited early by DuPont Chemical Company in Delaware, which had identified Kirby as an African American male working toward the Ph.D. They kept up with him throughout his graduate work, and when Kirby finished he went immediately to DuPont and stayed there. Unfortunately, Kirby died in 1991 of a massive heart attack. Roger McGinnis experienced a bit more difficulty getting into the career he wished to pursue. He worked initially at Phillips Petroleum in Oklahoma, then went to the state of Washington, where he currently is teaching. Bobby Lee Wilson did an excellent job of research, and to my great surprise he took up a teaching and research position in the Department of Chemistry at Texas Southern University in Houston. I always thought it was ironic that he went to Texas Southern and Kirby took industrial work. Bobby has excelled in his work at Texas Southern, moving to a point where he has published many papers and been responsible for many students going on to graduate study. Bobby was also the one who nominated me for the Henry A. Hill Lectureship Award, offered by the American Chemical Society's Northeast Section through the National Organization of Black Chemists and Chemical Engineers. I received that award in 1984. Bobby Lee was chair of the Department of Chemistry, then associate dean of the College of Arts and Sciences, and now vice president for Academic Affairs at Texas Southern. He manages to be active in research while taking on administrative duties.

I finally made the decision not to take on any more graduate students. I continued my association with chemistry as a teaching professor, rather than as a research professor. That was a major decision, and I made it reluctantly. My administrative work was causing me difficulty, but I was also not pleased with my progress as a professor in the Department of Chemistry. In neither case was I given any major orientation about what was expected of me in my new duties. I had no role models or mentors at MSU—neither in chemistry nor in administration, where the competition was no less keen. I struggled in chemistry in the earlier years. I drew mainly on my own experiences. Mentors who had served me so well during the years when I was a student were not available.

I had begun my assignment as assistant professor of chemistry in September 1969. Walter Adams, a professor of economics, had assumed the presidency of MSU at the beginning of 1969, following the retirement of John Hannah, who had accepted a position in the federal government in Washington, D.C. It was of some significance to me personally that my arrival at MSU coincided with President Adams's tenure and with the presence on the Board of Trustees of Don Stevens. Don had a long-term commitment to access and to equal opportunity through his work in labor unions within the state of Michigan. I believe both Adams and Stevens strongly influenced my appointment as an assistant professor in chemistry. In addition, by now Robert L. Green had assumed leadership for the Center for Urban Affairs, and he pressed vigorously to increase the numbers of African Americans on the MSU faculty.

During this period the Black Faculty and Administrators Association (BFAA) was established at Michigan State. I was at the organizational meeting where Irvin Vance, then associate professor of mathematics, was elected co-chairperson. The meeting took place in a special purpose room of Crossroads Cafeteria. Present was a campus visitor at the time, Benjamin Mays, president emeritus of Morehouse College within the Atlanta University Center. Few more distinguished African American scholars have visited Michigan State University. The BFAA still exists and has played a role in pressing the university to recruit more African American students and to hire more African American faculty and staff. While I was a founding member and initial co-chair (with Irvin Vance) of the BFAA, I must observe that my membership and active interest declined over the years. This occurred for several reasons. For one, the group included few faculty and more staff and administrators, especially in later years. In addition, the group tended to be led by whomever was the outspoken African American leader on campus. Robert L. Green was that leader during his tenure at MSU. He was widely respected among African American faculty and staff. Bob made frequent presentations before the Board of Trustees on issues affecting African Americans at MSU. Usually these were made independent of the BFAA. BFAA did not have formal status at MSU in the sense of being a part of the governance structure. It was a structured organization, however, with elected officers and regular meetings. It was also effective and would become even more so in later years.

The African American and African students had their organizations on the campus and not uncommonly worked on agendas of common interest. Among some of these student leaders were Ron Bailey, June Thomas, Richard Thomas, Barry Amis, Stan McClinton, and Michael Hudson. Two African students stand out—Kamuyu Wakengethe and Mina Kenyatti, both from East Africa. Kamuyu subsequently returned to Kenya and earned his Ph.D. Mina was a more radical student. He, too, returned to Kenya but was imprisoned for his antigovernment views. Both Kamuyu and Mina now reside in the United States. Not uncommonly, Kamuyu or Mina addressed African American students whenever they assembled in large groups for presentations or to discuss issues.

Perhaps the best indication of common interest between African and African American students was the sit-in at the African Studies

Center in 1969, when the staff was away at an international meeting in Canada. The students lacked confidence in the leadership of the center and did not feel the center reflected sufficient participation of either Africans or African Americans. They occupied the building in protest for several days. A few years later a Nigerian, Alfred Opubor, became the center's director.

Still another example was the Wilson Hall protest by African American students, who alleged mistreatment of African American dormitory employees by their white supervisors. The students and others occupied Wilson Hall Cafeteria for several days and nights. In response, President Walter Adams appointed a committee of faculty and staff to hold hearings on the grievances and to point the way toward some effective resolution. The group included me, Irvin Vance, Robert Underwood, Emery Foster (associate or assistant vice president for business and finance), and Milton Dickerson (vice president for student affairs). The student delegation included both African and African American representatives: Michael Hudson, Ron Bailey, Sam Riddle, Mina Kenyatti, and Stan McClinton (also known as Kimathi Muhammed). We met day and night to resolve the issue. One can never say what effect an event such as this has in the long run. In the short term, the public hearings were referred to in Academic Council as a kangaroo court. That they were not. The university made and continues to make significant progress in diversifying the staff in the residence hall system.

▼   ▼   ▼

In 1970, my third year at MSU, Dr. Clifton Wharton, Jr., became the first African American to assume the presidency of a major predominantly white university in the United States. I began a full year of service on the group appointed by President Wharton, the Commission on Admissions and Student Body Composition, to establish university policy in these areas. Dr. Ira Polley, former superintendent of public instruction for the state of Michigan, assumed executive directorship of this commission, whose membership was broadly based. We met regularly throughout the calendar year in several subcommittees. I served on the Subcommittee on the Disadvantaged because of my work with minority students in the Department of Chemistry. Project TAC, a year old at that time, had quickly earned a reputation on campus and had given me visibility in central administration. The work on this commission gave me a much broader orientation to MSU. It provided access to the president of the university, to faculty, to students, and even to alumni and friends of MSU. We developed a concise yet detailed report for the president on admissions policy and student body composition. The report functioned as a working document for the next 10 years in determining institutional policy in admissions.

Several individuals who served on the commission subsequently assumed major responsibility for carrying out recommendations contained in the report. Ira Polley became assistant provost for admissions and records; Dorothy Arata became assistant provost for undergraduate programs; and I became assistant provost for special programs, replacing Professor Robert Green as the only African American on the provost's staff.

The report of the commission called for increased admission of handicappers, minorities, older students, and women to Michigan State. It also called for the university to provide access for students who were economically and educationally disadvantaged. One can see in the report the definition of the newly created post of assistant provost for special programs. The report examined the need to provide academic support services on a systematic and sustained basis. There were also references to Honors students as well as the general student body, all of which fit into the mission of the university. This document led to the creation of greater access to MSU for African Americans, Hispanics, Native Americans, and Asian Americans, as well as for the handicapped.

▼   ▼   ▼

By the beginning of 1971 Ruth was pregnant with our second child. We subsequently moved from our duplex on Ann Street in

East Lansing to a three-bedroom white colonial at 5165 Brookfield Drive. (We later learned we had moved to Meridian Township and the Okemos School District.) We rented a truck and moved everything in a day and an evening, including Bramlett, who lay asleep in his crib.

We thoroughly enjoyed our new home on Brookfield and made many new and lasting friends in the neighborhood, among them the Washington family, who lived two houses north of us. John was a minister in the United Church of Christ, and Shirley was a teacher at Okemos High School. They had three fine sons—Jim, Gary, and Stuart—at various stages of schooling from elementary to high school. We spent many wonderful hours together, and our children, despite the distance in ages, came to know and love one another. We lived on Brookfield for seven years.

▼   ▼   ▼

In January 1971 Provost John E. Cantlon asked me to assume an administrative position with responsibility for programs for disadvantaged and handicapper students. I met subsequently with Provost Cantlon and President Wharton to discuss the job description for the position, which carried the title of assistant provost for Special Programs. I had the option of working under President Wharton or Provost John Cantlon. At the time, I was a relatively inexperienced assistant professor of chemistry whose career goal was to become a tenured professor. I did not consider the long-term prospects of an administrative position. I opted to remain under the provost, who had responsibility for academic affairs within the institution. This was a significant decision, considering how much I could have learned working in close association with an individual such as President Wharton, who went on to become chancellor of the State University of New York System; president and chairman of the board of TIAA-CREF, one of America's largest insurance companies; and then U.S. assistant secretary of state!

In any case, I was quite interested in this position because of the perspective it would provide on the university. I must admit that I have always enjoyed having a view of the "bigger picture," and this position promised to provide that. When I joined the provost's staff, I became its only African American administrator. There were many other individuals on the staff, and we met weekly. Initially the others included the director of institutional research, Paul Dressel; the associate provost for academic planning, John Dietrich; the assistant provost for instructional development, Robert Davis; the assistant provost for undergraduate programs, Dorothy Arata; the assistant provost for admissions and records, Ira Polley; the assistant provost for health programs, Bob Schuetz; and the assistant provost for administration, Herman King. In my initial role I had no direct link with the academic governance system and would only slowly become aware of its importance at Michigan State.

My immediate charge was to assume responsibility for programs for disadvantaged and handicapper students. I learned that there was an existing program for disadvantaged students, the Center for Supportive Services, located in the Union Building. It had its own director and a staff of four professionals. While there was no program for the handicapped, there was an individual who would play a major role in orienting me to this dimension of my responsibilities—Judy Taylor (later Gentile). I had a budget of $123,000 with which to carry out my tasks.

When I hired my office staff, I experienced immediate pressure from the provost to hire a secretary who was already in place in the College of Communication. The dean of that college was leaving, and the new dean wanted to choose his own secretary. Provost Cantlon asked that I interview this secretary with the view of hiring her; if I did so, the provost would pay the salary. I considered the matter carefully. I interviewed the secretary, but I had long since concluded that this would be one important decision that I must make. I had every intention of hiring my own secretary, and I did. I had to fund the position out of my own limited resources. I hired Delores Reed, an African American, who was then a secretary in James Madison College. We occupied conference room 443A on the fourth floor of the Administration Building.

I met with personnel in the Center for Supportive Services. The director, Henry C. Johnson, a quite competent African American, was aided by additional staff. The main service provided by the center at this time was tutoring. Charles Thornton, an African American, had the responsibility for that aspect of the program. The staff also provided counseling and saw themselves, in part, as academic counselors for students. When I asked for data, I learned that little was systematically available on the students being served by the program. I was most disappointed, but I learned that data were flowing from Institutional Research to a graduate student in the center, who was employed by the Center for Urban Affairs. One of my first goals, then, was to develop and get control of a data base from which the Center for Supportive Services could function. Requests to Institutional Research for data led to an interesting development. An associate director suggested to me that in my new role I should be the individual who received all data on minority students. This suggestion surprised me, for my responsibilities did not include all minorities. Nonetheless, I put myself into the position to receive these data regularly, or to authorize the receipt of the data by others who might request it. The new office now regularly gathered information which the staff used to monitor the academic progress of the developmental students. The program moved along well and continued to provide the basic services that it had provided so well to the students in its charge.

All of the students served had been admitted under the Developmental Program, or the "Detroit Project." As of 1971 only 300 students had been admitted to the university through this program. The number would shortly double. The students were entering MSU with GPAs in the 2.4-2.8 range and a minimum SAT score of 800, the criteria I had used for Project TAC. This had occurred following a meeting I had with the former vice president for special projects, Gordon Sabine. He had heard about the success of Project TAC and wanted to know more about it from me. In fall 1971, with the admission of 300 or more students under the Detroit Project, MSU began receiving many African American students who were underprepared in their work in high school. There were other African Americans entering MSU independent of the Detroit Project. Thus began a broadening of access for African Americans and later for other minorities, particularly Hispanics. The intent was to meet the students' academic support needs via programs in the Center for Supportive Services and via various remedial and developmental courses available in the curriculum. There was very little going on within traditional departments through the faculty to help these students, who came to MSU with high hopes, but only 40-50 percent in any entering class ever earned a bachelor's degree at MSU. The others left for various reasons, mostly academic. While these were all presumably educationally disadvantaged students, and many were economically disadvantaged as well, they were also mainly Hispanics and African Americans, at least from 1967 to 1970. From 1971 on, as the number admitted rose to 300 or more each fall term, the proportion of Hispanics declined, and African Americans dominated.

The office serving handicapper students also needed attention. My first step was to hire Judy Taylor as a graduate assistant to help me in this respect. We did have some existing services, but they were meager. For example, there was a transport system that consisted of a van (leased from the Motor Pool) and a wooden lift that had to be manually put in place. There were not many students at this time needing such transportation, and if there were, they must have provided their own, as we were in no position to serve them. For the blind there were sound-proofed reading rooms in the MSU Library staffed by volunteers from Tower Guard, a service honorary. At this time the main focus was on services for handicappers in wheelchairs, as they had the greatest need. Judy Taylor had been in a wheelchair since the age of eight, when she was stricken with polio. We created the program for handicappers virtually from scratch.

I learned that a major program for handicappers at the University of California at Berkeley provided services from a community base to many veterans, and I decided to visit the program. I was trying to decide on whom to hire as the first director of the Office of Programs for Handicapper Students. The two major candidates were Judy Taylor and Dixie Dumbrausky, a state of Michigan vocational rehabilitation counselor, who dealt with the needs of the handicapped at MSU. She was not handicapped. The program at Berkeley was run by a veteran operating from a wheelchair, and there were many handicappers visible at the center on the two days I spent there in summer 1972. I came back from California convinced that the person I should hire to run this program was Judy Taylor. Hiring her was not to be an easy task.

I initially attempted to appoint Judy as an Administrative Professional under the university's regular personnel system. Prospective employees had to take a physical examination, which Judy passed initially. The Personnel Office rejected that decision, considering her incapable of carrying out the job assignment. The Personnel Office insisted that Judy undergo a second physical examination, and this physician found that she was "not able to undertake the work responsibility." Of course, I was committed to Judy and quite upset. I went directly to President Wharton with this matter, and I advised him that we were encountering discrimination against the handicapped (there was then no federal law forbidding it). President Wharton immediately called Keith Groty, then assistant vice president for personnel, who was engaged in contract negotiations. The Personnel Office remained recalcitrant, and we appointed Judy not under the AP system but under the Specialist system, which was used for faculty personnel. This meant that the Office of Programs for Handicappers had a different classification of employees than the Office of Supportive Services. Judy and I worked closely together over the next two decades and developed a major new thrust for the handicapped at Michigan State University.

In 1971 Ruth's mother, Ella Ruth Simms, paid a visit to us from her home in Savannah, as Ruth was expecting our second child. In the late evening of August 25, 1971, Ruth came down the stairs and said she thought it was time to go to the hospital. This child was anxious to enter the world, and she was born early on Thursday morning, August 26, 1971. Like my son, she was a large child at birth, weighing more than nine pounds. She was a lovely young lady, and we were quite excited to have been blessed with a son and a daughter. I can still remember all the photographs we took, including one with Bramlett, then three years old, reaching out to touch his new sister. We named her after her maternal great-grand-mother, Priscilla Simms, which was also Ruth's middle and family name.

Priscilla was to get another name several days later, when we held a very large naming ceremony for her in the tradition of West Africa. Several of our West African friends had suggested that we have the ceremony, among them some Ghanaians, including John Nabila. The tradition is to hold the naming ceremony shortly after a child is born and to have it in association with the child's "first outing."

Ruth and I agreed and issued invitations. Ceremonial slaughter of an animal was required, and the students searched diligently for a goat but could not find one in the greater Lansing area. They settled on a white rooster. When the day finally came, we were expecting well over a hundred people. We had invited most of our friends from chemistry and sociology, from the provost's staff, from across the greater Lansing community. In our huge backyard the guests mingled—African American and white alike, American and foreign. It was truly a great occasion. All of the family wore either dashikis or other traditional African dress. The kenti cloth was very evident, and the Nigerian women in their sophisticated high head-dress were striking. It was an impressive sight to behold.

African students performed the ceremony. Two Ghanaians, John Nabila and John Afesi, played major roles. I cannot fully describe the ritual because they used West African languages at certain points. It took on traditional Ghanaian characteristics, with some addition of the Muslim traditions of northern Nigeria. They had Priscilla taste various spices—sugar, salt, pepper, and others—each with a symbolic meaning. Priscilla was given the additional name of Lamisi, meaning a woman born on a Thursday. It was truly a lovely ceremony carried out in a very dignified manner. Afterward, we had traditional African drumming done by those there. I will forever remember the picture of Ruth holding Priscilla Lamisi, kneeling in the grass, while John Nabila, John Afesi, and others carried out the ceremony.

We now had a lovely daughter in our family—Priscilla Lamisi Simms Hamilton—who we knew would go on to do great things and make herself and her family proud. To our dear friends, John and Kathy Hunter, Priscilla would forever be Lamisi. John had done substantial work in Ghana years earlier; John Nabila was pursuing a Ph.D. at Michigan State under Professor Hunter's direction. What I did not know at this time, but learned later, is that John and I would become lasting friends, and by that I mean both Johns—John Nabila and John Hunter. I also did not know, but soon realized, that Ruth and I would make a trip to Africa together in little more than a year from that September.

Our daughter and our son continued to grow and to mature, and we became a closely knit family of four.

▼   ▼   ▼

By the end of 1971, Delores Reed and I had moved into permanent office space in the Administration Building adjacent to the assistant provost for undergraduate programs, Dorothy Arata. Judy Taylor and I were well on the path of building a centralized office of programs for handicapper students, and I had become more integrally involved in the day-to-day management of the Office of Supportive Services. Meanwhile, my work with Chuck Gordon on a gubernatorial task force had led to a new contact, Clark Chipman. Clark was a regional program officer of the U.S. Department of Education. I had also learned about the Michigan Council of Educational Opportunity Programs (EOP). I received an invitation from Chuck Gordon, an African American, to attend a training workshop for EOP directors at the University of Iowa. At this gathering I would meet many individuals who would become very important in MSU's efforts to obtain federal funding for its academic support programs for disadvantaged and handicapper students. Among them were Arnold Mitchem, also an African American, who was director of TRIO programs at Marquette University in Milwaukee; Clara Fitzpatrick, an African American, assistant director of the College Board, located in Evanston,

Illinois; Clark Chipman, who I have already mentioned; and Manuel Pierson, an African American, who was director of the Upward Bound program at Oakland University in Michigan. Our host for this meeting was Phil Jones, an African American.

Among other things we discussed "management by objectives" and its importance in the federal TRIO programs: Upward Bound, Talent Search, and Special Services for Disadvantaged Students. We also began discussions on where we were going with these programs regionally and nationally. We laid the foundation at this meeting for the Mid-America Association of Educational Opportunity Program Personnel (MAEOPP), which ultimately encompassed Michigan, Wisconsin, Ohio, Indiana, Illinois, and Iowa. Most of those engaged in planning in Iowa were African Americans, but there were also whites, Native Americans, and Hispanics. On this occasion the people who built MAEOPP became associates. We were being tested by older hands to determine what we might contribute and whether we would do it.

I also learned a great deal about federal funding and how to seek it for programs for the disadvantaged and handicapped at MSU. I had already submitted a proposal for a Special Services for Disadvantaged Students Program to the U.S. Department of Education and was awaiting a decision. Michigan State had sought funding from the federal government in previous years but had been unsuccessful. I had seen a copy of that earlier proposal, which had asked for a large amount of money. It had been developed by Gordon Sabine, vice president for special projects, who also had responsibility for admissions and had established the original Detroit Project. Dr. Gwen Norrell initially administered that project through MSU's Counseling Center.

Vice President Sabine had alienated people in Washington, D.C., and Michigan State University was persona non grata on that scene. Sabine had gone over the head of the director of the program to get funding for a veterans' Talent Search, which he took to Vietnam. It was a good effort on his part but a "no-no" as far as the Washington bureaucracy was concerned. He had used the wrong approach. In our proposal we had sought funding for disadvantaged students, and we were successful. I am convinced that this was due in part to the contacts I had established at the Iowa meeting. These programs and the funding decisions at this time were regionalized, and Clark Chipman had the final say.

Three factors made the probability quite high that MSU's program would be funded. First, it was a quality proposal. Second, very few people with Ph.D.s were involved with TRIO programs on the national level, particularly with Ph.D.s in respected disciplines and on the faculty within their institutions. I met that criterion. Third, there was great interest in getting a large university involved with TRIO programs. At this time neither the University of Michigan nor MSU had received any funding under the Special Services for Disadvantaged Students Program. Although we did have an Upward Bound program, there was discontent regionally with that program and its director. Effective July 1, 1973, we received $89,000 from the U.S. Department of Education's Special Services for Disadvantaged Students Program. The grant assured the doubling of the effort that we expended on students from disadvantaged backgrounds. (From 1973-1989 we would bring more than $4 million in federal funding to MSU from the U.S. Department of Education.)

The proposal did not call for full integration of our Center for Supportive Services into the new program; instead of a merger, we established a separate unit and located it in Holden Hall. This was how 1973 ended, with Michigan State having two programs to serve students from disadvantaged backgrounds—one institutionally funded and one federally funded.

▼   ▼   ▼

My involvement with Clark Chipman, Chuck Gordon, and others in EOP represented a substantial experience in my administrative life. These programs, particularly once I was operating with a funded Special Program for Students from Disadvantaged Backgrounds, would occupy my attention for the next 20 years and more. Because of these contacts, I became a member of the Region V TRIO Programs Advisory Council, which was created during the tenure of Dr. Peter Mousolite as director of the regional office. When I served on the council, the director was Clark Chipman, an outspoken, liberal, white male who was very aggressively support-ive of TRIO programs. I made frequent trips—almost monthly—to meetings of the council, which at the time was chaired by Charles Gordon. We met at the YMCA College on Wacker Drive in down-town Chicago. Our meetings focused on the annual conference of project directors held at The Abbey in Fontana, Wisconsin. We began to lay the foundation for greater involvement beyond the TRIO Advisory Council through a regional association of EOP per-sonnel. I enjoyed my work with this group, which was about to form a new regional and later a national association. For one, it brought me much more closely in contact with African American professionals in higher education but without the Ph.D. degree. They also were much fun to work with, and our business meetings invariably allowed the opportunity for social interaction. Through them I would meet many other people around the country, includ-ing Hispanics, Native Americans, and whites, involved with expanding educational opportunity in universities.

The leadership of the TRIO Advisory Council passed from Chuck Gordon to Arnold Mitchem in the early 1970s. It was under Arnold's leadership that we made the transition to the association in fall 1974. I learned a great deal from the council about organiza-tions and how to build one. I also learned, or would learn, a great deal about the federal government, how laws are passed, how bills are written, and how one goes about influencing people in the administration and in the Congress to the benefit of one's institu-tion or state. It would be a phenomenal experience. It would also take its toll on me. The EOP people worked for long hours when-ever they met, much beyond the normal meeting time, and covered topics that extended beyond the formal agenda. For example, at a regional TRIO Advisory Council meeting we would hold a formal session only to adjourn to have a meal and then meet that evening and on into the morning hours, in the room of Clark Chipman, Clara Fitzpatrick, or others. This was a pattern I had seen emerge at the Iowa discussions. There, too, we had a formal agenda that we followed during the day, but then the evening discussions would go on and on and on. I did not know what to make of it at first. I wondered why people expended their energies in this way, but as I saw ideas shift and change and new ideas begin to grow and take shape, I realized what this expenditure of energy was all about, and I was pleased to be a part of it. I was fascinated by this group of paraprofessionals seeking to organize themselves into an association. While my primary purpose was to secure funding for MSU programs, I also was encouraged by the respect shown me by members of this group. I was beginning to feel that I was part of something that could have an effect on the education of minorities not only at MSU but also across the state of Michigan and even nationally. For their own reasons—namely, to have someone involved who had formal academic credentials and who was from a major institution—the group also catered to me somewhat and pressed me to become more deeply involved with them.

At Michigan State we obtained additional funding from the Region V Office for not only the Special Services for Disadvantaged Students Program but also for the handicapper component. This allowed the formal kickoff for the program for the handicapped at Michigan State University under the leadership of Judy Taylor. Clark Chipman again played a major role in the award of this grant, for which we had submitted a quality proposal.

Chipman was helpful to us in other ways. At this time there was considerable attention to program evaluation within the region and at the national level. There had never been an evaluation model developed for Special Services for Disadvantaged Students Programs. At MSU I approached Dr. Gwen Norrell of the Counseling Center regarding whether she knew any promising graduate students who might work with me for a year or two on such a project. It was in this manner that I met Frank Vivio in 1974, who was pursuing his Ph.D. in higher education and had a strong background in evaluation and measurement. Together we developed a proposal to the U.S. Office of Education seeking funding for an evaluation model for Special Programs for Students from Disadvantaged Backgrounds. From Clark Chipman we received encouragement and financial support. Within a year we published the model as a booklet and disseminated copies free of charge to every special services program in the country. We believed this book went a long way toward helping put projects on a firm foundation in terms of evaluation. In addition, the quality of proposals submitted to Washington increased.

A final project that Frank undertook with institutional support was a survey of all TRIO programs within the state of Michigan, perhaps the first and only study of its sort. We gathered much good information. The study was conducted under the auspices of the Michigan Council of Educational Opportunity Programs (later the Michigan Chapter of the Mid-America Association of Educational Opportunity Program Personnel). Shortly after this project was completed, Frank earned his degree and moved on to the East West Center in Honolulu, Hawaii, as an assistant director. Our paths would cross again.

We had at this time two very different staffs in the Office of Supportive Services and in the Special Services for Disadvantaged Students Program (SSDSP). In the former, the personnel were nearly all African American when I came on board; Henry Johnson was director and had an African American secretary, and Charles Thornton, Maggie Martin, and, later, Florence Harris were on the staff. When we received funding for the SSDSP, I hired Henry Braddock, an African American, as director, and he built up a more diverse staff, including Harvey Jariell, III, an African American male; Sylvia Jackson, an African American female; Laura Shiro, an Asian American female; and Bertram Green, a white male. Thus began a period of increased diversity among those providing academic support services through these two programs. They were a very creative and dedicated group. The two staffs did have different charges. The center served students admitted under the Detroit Project, while the federally funded SSDSP was to serve low-income students irrespective of racial/ethnic background. In reality, even the latter served a largely African American student population and smaller numbers of students from other racial/ethnic groups.

The Office of Supportive Services and the SSDSP continued to function as separate and distinct programs, but I knew that at some point I would need to merge them. I should also note that when the federally funded SSDSP was established we appointed staff not under the Administrative Professional system but under the Specialist system, again following the approach adopted with the handicapper program and Judy Taylor. This created difficulties that had not been anticipated. In 1974 the university mounted a Hayes Study of its Administrative Professional system, and staff in the Center for Supportive Services had to participate. When the study was completed, no one on campus was happy, and the center's staff was particularly disturbed. All of them had been classified as AP 8 advisors, the same classification as admissions officers. They wanted and had sought a higher classification. The salary levels were also a matter of concern.

We deliberated considerably on this topic, and finally I put forward the reappointment of all personnel in the center under the Specialist system. This was as much out of frustration with the Personnel Office and their reclassification scheme as anything else. I thought that this would be better for the staff than the AP system. I knew it would be better to deal with one personnel office for our professional employees than to deal with two. I did not anticipate the strong reaction from the center's staff. While they were not happy with the AP classification, they did not want to forgo their appointments within that system. The AP system was perceived as providing job security that the Specialist system did not immediately grant. This was the beginning of a time of trouble for me with staff in the various offices, and the result would be some profound changes in the units over the next several years.

▼   ▼   ▼

The end of 1972 found me concerned with other matters as my wife and I planned a trip with our son to West Africa. We would be in Ghana and West Africa for more than seven weeks beginning in early December. Ruth had encouraged me to write in advance to the University of Ghana that I would be visiting in my capacity as an assistant provost for special programs. I was hesitant to do this. I had never traveled abroad on my own before; Ruth had, and I should have taken her suggestion. I was very nervous about the trip, which required leaving our daughter, who was only sixteen months old; Ruth flew to Savannah to leave Priscilla with her grandmother. When Ruth returned to Lansing, we departed for New York. From there we left for Ghana, stopping in London and Sierra Leone. The thought of separating my family like that unnerved me at the time and would always cause me problems.

Ruth had done her research for the Ph.D. in Ghana in the 1960s, studying market women's organizations in an urban setting, and had written a book on urbanization in West Africa. Bramlett was only five years old and in kindergarten. How much of the trip he can recall I do not know. Although it was a joy to have him with us, I sorely missed our lovely daughter.

I should note that we initially had great difficulty getting visas to enter Sierra Leone. I do not know why, but we did. So we had set out without visas. While in London we took a chance and stopped at the office of the High Commissioner for Sierra Leone and obtained the visas. I was glad of that, as you will see later. In Freetown I was immediately struck by the military presence—lots of men in uniform carrying automatic weapons. They insisted upon searching our luggage and were brusque about it. I was so pleased that we had not entered the country without visas! I still wonder to this day what would have happened if we had. From there we took a ferry across the river to the city of Freetown and our hotel. We had a fine stay and spent a good deal of time with Dr. Enid Forde, a Sierra Leonean and a professor at the University of Freetown. Enid, who had studied at Northwestern, was a very dear friend of Ruth and had been a guest at our wedding. We also met the parents of Daphne Williams, who was a graduate student at MSU and sometimes babysat with Bramlett and Priscilla. They prepared a wonderful dinner for us at their home. I remember that we took a taxi there, and upon arrival our cab was in a minor accident with another. There followed a loud argument between the two drivers, a crowd quickly gathered, and some of the bystanders began to contribute to the argument. Meanwhile, Daphne quietly led Ruth and me into the house, and the argument went on for some time. Daphne Williams ultimately earned her Ph.D. at MSU and is now a professor at Wayne State University in Detroit, Michigan. She married George

Ntiri, a Ghanaian, and our daughter, Priscilla Lamisi, was the flower girl at their wedding.

Outside the Faculty Club at the University of Freetown I saw my first grapefruit tree, laden with fruit. I was an urban youth and not accustomed to such sights. Africa was lush, and as I looked about at the people of Freetown when we walked its streets, there was no question in my mind that most African Americans had originated in West Africa. So many people looked just like people I had seen in Chicago, particularly in my childhood.

We flew from Freetown to Accra, Ghana, and from there went by automobile to the University of Ghana at Legon. We were met at the airport in Accra by some of the market women with whom Ruth had worked while conducting dissertation research. They wanted to see Ruth's husband and her son. We were also met by Ruth's friends Dorothy and Sanni Thomas. A Nigerian by birth, he was the former head of the offices of the military training school in Ghana and now head of the country's State Hotels Corporation. Dorothy, a nurse, was the representative for a U.S. pharmaceutical firm. They brought many groceries, beer, and other refreshments to tide us over for our first week and took us on to Legon. Others at the airport were John Nabila and Joe Geki, each of whom received a Ph.D. from MSU, and both had been involved in the naming ceremony for Priscilla Lamisi Simms Hamilton.

Ghana was a lovely country I thought, full of friendly people; I was not disappointed during my entire stay. This was the place from which many of our ancestors had come, not of their bidding, hundreds of years earlier. We resided in the Ford Foundation's Fellows Flats at the university. Parenthetically, I should note that if I had taken Ruth's advice and written to the university's vice chancellor in advance, we would have stayed in a faculty flat. Nonetheless, we were quite comfortable, particularly after I got accustomed to the lizards running up and down the walls of our bedroom and living room. They were harmless things, and they did not seem to bother our son, who was absolutely fascinated with them. Ruth had arranged for a young African teenager to be with us to take care of our son, and for an interpreter, a car, and a driver. This was not a vacation for Ruth, but a follow-up on research begun ten years earlier. For me it was pure vacation.

James Hamilton (left) and brother, Howard, 1943.

Elementary school photo, 1944. James Hamilton top row, first on left.

Hamilton's maternal grandmother, Emma Jones, ca. 1940s.

Hamilton's maternal grandfather, James L. Jones.

Hamilton's paternal grandmother, Alice Foster, ca. 1940s.

Maude Hamilton, mother of James Hamilton, ca. 1950s.

Maude Hamilton Posey and Harry (Scottie) Posey, ca. 1979.

Hamilton's father, Howard (right) and grandfather James Jones.

Hamilton with the
Fifth Marines in
Korea, 1954.

Hamilton with the
Marines at Camp
Pendleton, 1953.

Hamilton ran the
laundry for the
Second Battalion,
Fifth Marines.
Korean women were
hired to wash
clothes.

Ruth Priscilla Simms Hamilton and James Hamilton on their wedding day, July 3, 1965, in Savannah, Georgia.

Hamilton's daughter, Priscilla "Lamisi" Simms Hamilton and Benji Ishaku at her African naming ceremony, September 1971.

Ruth, holding Priscilla; and James Hamilton.

John Nabila (left) and Henry Wellbeck, Ghanaian graduate students who planned and coordinated the naming ceremony.

Ruth, Priscilla, James, and Bramlett Hamilton, 1977.

James Hamilton dances with daughter, Priscilla, at a classmate's "quinceañera," 1988.

Bramlett and James Hamilton, 1987.

Bramlett, Maude Hamilton Posey, Priscilla, James, and Ruth prior to Priscilla's Okemos High School graduation ceremony, 1989.

Priscilla, Bramlett, and James after Bramlett's MSU graduation ceremony, 1989.

James with Bramlett at Bramlett's 1992 graduation from Stanford University Law School.

James Hamilton (far right), TRIO Day, February 1986. TRIO refers to the original three federally funded educational opportunity programs—Upward Bound, Talent Search, and Student Support Services—for low-income first generation, and handicapper students. Courtesy of Office of Supportive Services, MSU.

MSU students and staff marching on campus in celebration of TRIO Day, February 1986. Courtesy of Office of Supportive Services, MSU.

TRIO students marching on MSU Campus, TRIO Day 1988. Courtesy of Office of Supportive Services, MSU.

MSU TRIO students at the Lansing Civic Center, 1988. Courtesy of Office of Supportive Services, MSU.

James Hamilton addresses students from the steps of the state Capitol, Lansing. TRIO Day, 1988. Courtesy of Office of Supportive Services, MSU.

James Hamilton (standing, far right) with a class of minority undergraduate Summer Research Opportunity Program participants. The program began in 1986. Courtesy of Office of Supportive Services, MSU.

The "Professors Hamilton" at MSU commencement exercises, 1985.

James Hamilton presents an award to Gwen Norrell, MSU professor and founder of the Detroit Project, 1987, at the Office of Supportive Services Honors and Appreciation Reception.

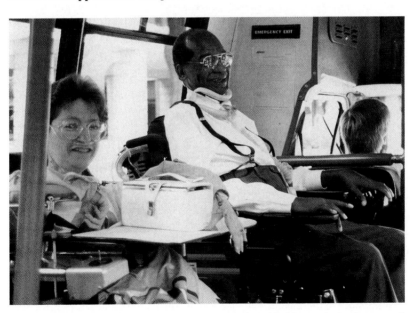

Judy Gentile, director of the Office of Programs for Handicapper Students, and James Hamilton aboard MSU transportation system for handicappers, 1991.

Mid-America Association of Educational Opportunity Program Personnel (MAEOPP) Salute to Dr. James B. Hamilton, Chicago, May 24, 1990. From left to right: Clark Chipman, George Jackson, Arnold Mitchum, James Hamilton, Clarence Shelly, Charles (Chuck) Gordon, Win Stone, Rozelle Boyd, and Clifford Brooks. Courtesy of MAEOPP.

MSU staff at MAEOPP Salute, 1990. Left to right: Viciki Dukelow, Glenda Hammond, Lonnie Eiland, Florence Harris, Ira Washington, James Hamilton, Delores C. Reed, Mary Lee Vance, Deborah Galvan, and Betty Sanford. Courtesy of MAEOPP.

Provost David Scott, Ruth, and Bramlett with James Hamilton at MSU reception in his honor, 1991. Courtesy of MSU Department of Human Relations.

James Hamilton with members of Alpha Phi Alpha at MSU reception, 1991.

James and Ruth Hamilton at Alpha Chi Boule (Lansing chapter of Sigma Pi Phi fraternity) Christmas party, 1993.

I went with Ruth everywhere as she pursued her work with the market women. They were a friendly and open group of people. We were entertained in the home of Ayo Deidei by other market women friends of hers, who sang to us. One woman accompanied them on a fascinating instrument, which I admired and which we then received as a gift.

The campus of the University of Ghana at Legon was particularly impressive. I had long before studied the connections between the history of Ghana and the United Negro Improvement Association, established several decades earlier by Marcus Garvey, a Jamaican and Black Nationalist who had started a shipping fleet called the Black Star Line. Its symbol had been adopted by Kwame Nkrumah, first president of Ghana, when the country became independent. The Black Star was on the four sides of the campanile at the university and on the Ghanaian flag; there was a Black Star Square and a Black Star Park, where national celebrations were held. It is good to know one's history, most particularly when you have to gather it on your own rather than in school.

One fascinating sight to me in Ghana was tall mounds of dirt visible everywhere, even in the center of the city. They were termite mounds, six feet tall. The sculpture dominated the landscape of Ghana!

Traveling in Ghana was quite an experience no matter how it was done. Each day that Ruth and I set out to visit one of the many groups with which she worked, it was an excursion for the full day. It took quite a bit of time just to get into downtown Legon, and getting around the city was difficult. There were just too many cars, and the roads were just too narrow. We were to meet with one group late in the evening and dine with them. We left at 3:00 or 4:00 P.M., planning to arrive about 6:00 P.M., but by the time we got there, it was well past that. They were waiting in the full dress of their society, and they opened in traditional song for Ruth when she arrived. Their respect and affection for Ruth were shown in the ceremonial mask that they presented her.

My own travels took me to northern Ghana, at Ruth's insistence. Again, I had that reluctance to leave a part of my family and travel alone, but I did visit Tamale, passing through Kumasi. I flew on

Ghanaian Airways, which was quite an experience, as the people on the plane were in traditional dress and carried all kinds of goods and materials. In Tamale I was met by John Nabila's brother, who drove me up to Bolgatanga. We visited hospitals and other sights in the area, went shopping, and bought several fascinating local crafts. We were in the Muslim section of the country, and early on my first morning there I heard the call to prayer, repeated at different times during the day. Bolgatanga was the region where John Nabila had grown up, and it was a pleasure to have a chance to visit there and to see his home.

I took another side trip with our driver to visit the University of Cape Coast and to see Cape Coast Castle. The drive was one hell of an experience. The road, after a point, became two relatively narrow lanes with very poor shoulders. The driver tended to drive down the middle of the road, which did not help my nerves at all. His English was not very good, so I did not have the greatest company going down there. The university was quite large, different in appearance from the University of Ghana at Legon. It looked more tropical, with light-colored buildings and exterior shades to keep the sun out during the heat of the day. My major plan was to visit Sam Paton, a former student then in Ghana with the Peace Corps. Sam had earned his Ph.D. under Carl Brubaker in the Department of Chemistry at MSU. I had gotten to know him and his wife very well in East Lansing. Not knowing that Ruth and I were in Africa, Sam was shocked when he saw me, of course.

From the university I went to Cape Coast Castle, built by the Portuguese and used as a staging area during the slave trade. It was deeply moving to walk through the dark rooms in the lower part of the castle, where I saw the remains of chains and shackles that had been used on the African captives when they were waiting for the ships to take them to all parts of the Americas as slaves. The fishing village nearby was of particular interest because of the beautifully colored large boats with all of their markings. Fishing nets were thrown over the ground to dry. I sat there for hours watching the comings and goings of the fishing fleets. When the huge boats returned from the sea, they captured a wave as they got closer to shore and came in like surf boarders. I could see the helmsman standing in the rear of the boat, maintaining its balance, while the fishermen who handled the nets sat nearby. The women were on the shore, ready to take the fish and prepare them for market.

From Cape Coast we drove back to Accra, where I was reunited with my wife and son. We prepared for the trip home. Our visit to Africa, my first and my wife's second, was a fantastic experience. I looked forward someday to returning to Ghana, but even as I write this has not occurred. Ghana has had several coups and now is under the rule of Lt. Rawlings. It continues to go through troubling economic and political change, but the people and the country remain spirited and forward looking. The memory of that trip, the return to the origins of the African Americans, will always be with me.

▼   ▼   ▼

The handicapper students' program at MSU had a very different beginning and would have a very different experience from the Office of Supportive Services. The latter primarily served minority students, whereas the Office of Programs for Handicapper Students, at least in the early days, served a white population. This should not be surprising, nor should the fact that the white students who were served during these early years came from advantaged backgrounds, although there were clear exceptions, such as the director of the program, Judy Taylor. The diversity of the program changed over the years as awareness of accessibility for handicappers spread across the state and as individuals from less advantaged backgrounds, irrespective of race or gender, found their way to Michigan State.

The state of Michigan had a long history of providing quality support services to handicappers, although in many instances through sheltered workshops. There was a base of support and interest for helping handicappers, and this was readily tapped within the state and at MSU. When we moved ahead with programs in the early 1970s, we had the support of the state, the university, and external agencies such as the Michigan Lions Club, the Michigan Trial

Lawyers Association, and the Office of Services for the Blind. Within a short time MSU modified its own policies to include access for handicappers and moved ahead with the assistance of the Office of Programs for Handicapper Students and other offices to make the campus more accessible. The state passed a law mandating access for handicappers well before the federal law was enacted.

In contrast, the Center for Supportive Services was working in difficult terrain. There was no clear support beyond the state or even within the state for disadvantaged students and minorities. On the contrary, there was a substantial amount of pessimism about the ability to remediate the educational problems of the underprepared minority students, particularly African Americans. During this period there was a major shift in national efforts to bring about equality in racial relations. Following the riots in the late 1960s and the death of Martin Luther King, Jr., who had put together a coalition of whites and African Americans in a nonviolent civil rights movement, a more radical leadership had emerged. The latter frightened the white community, which resorted to blaming African Americans for their own condition. Thus, the Center for Supportive Services had an uphill struggle. Even liberal faculty members were less anxious about the educational problems of the disadvantaged and the ability or the appropriateness of remedying their needs at a university such as MSU.

When I returned from Africa, I continued to work with the Office of Programs for Handicapper Students, the Center for Supportive Services, and the new Special Services for Disadvantaged Students Program to carry out the charge of my office. I had already begun to think about the need for more systematic information about what we were doing in these programs. I also moved to reorganize these units into the Office of Special Programs. In writing the first annual report on special programs, I used the occasion to comment on their history and emergence from the old Center for Urban Affairs. I also published data according to racial/ethnic background and according to the fall term in which Developmental Program students had been admitted.

In 1974 my report presented the first statistics showing the persistence and retention of developmental students from enrollment to graduation, which was 90 percent after the first year. That figure declined in subsequent years, reaching a low after the fifth or sixth year of 40-44 percent. These rates were lower than desired, but it was the best that could be achieved with the tutoring and counseling available through the Center for Supportive Services and other programs. Compared to Developmental Program students, regularly admitted African Americans during this time (and at present) had somewhat higher persistence rates, but even so these were lower than desired. African American students had greater difficulty realizing success at MSU than any other group, with the possible exception of Hispanics. Among the African Americans, women outnumbered men by three to two. This reflected the higher dropout rates for African American men in public schools in Michigan urban areas. Data also showed that African American women had a lower persistence rate to graduation than did African American males. These annual reports were difficult to put together, but we were able to do it with the assistance of data compiled for us by the Office of Institutional Research. I was also aided, for example, by the Office of Programs for Handicapper Students, which began to grow after we received the federal grant.

By 1974 there was a van with a hydraulic lift, and we had purchased a second vehicle, called a bussette. These transported up to 12 handicapped students to and from classes, a major change from the early days. In 1975 we purchased a transette, and this fleet of three vehicles functioned under a plan whereby we could replace one vehicle a year. The Office of Programs for Handicapper Students (OPHS) had also changed location. It had started out in Owen Graduate Center, in one of the rooms reserved for study. We used the space during the day for the handicapper office, and at night we locked up our telephone to avoid use by graduate students. This was clearly an inadequate situation, and we then moved to the MSU Library, to the reading room for the blind. This turned out to be an excellent idea, as it brought blind students more directly under the responsibility of OPHS. The program remained in the Library for several years. The transportation system also operated out of this facility, and when we installed radios in the vehicles, the original antenna was placed upon the MSU Library.

OPHS grew and developed under Judy Taylor's significant leadership, both on and off campus. She developed important contacts with the Michigan Office of Vocational Rehabilitation and Office of Services to the Blind. Ultimately, we purchased all new tapes and other equipment for use in the reading room for blind students. In her campus activity, Judy Taylor was aided early on by a graduate student, Eric Gentile. He was outgoing and aggressively concerned about the needs of the handicapped at MSU, particularly those who operated from wheelchairs. Eric could be abrasive, and he probably made more enemies than friends as he went about his business—the opposite was true for Judy Taylor. They were a pair, and they worked well together. The Board of Trustees knew them well, as Judy and Eric frequently made presentations before them regarding the needs of the handicapper population. Much of what we achieved at MSU was due to their strong advocacy. Later, Judy and Eric would wed.

That same spirit of advocacy was not as evident in the programs for disadvantaged students, and I often wondered why. One objective of the handicapper programs was advocacy, but this was not the case for the programs for disadvantaged students. I also never saw myself as a "leader of the people." That responsibility at MSU rested with Robert L. Green, director of the Center for Urban Affairs and very outspoken on minority student issues. It would have been difficult for anyone else to assume that role, even if they had wanted to, which I did not. Many of the African Americans on my staff admired Dr. Green for his outspokenness and probably wanted to see the same thing from me. But that was something I did not attempt to do, although I did try to stay in touch with the issues and to keep myself visible among the African American community. From my perspective, what we were doing in the programs that I administered would have a greater long-term effect on African American students and other minorities and handicappers than any of the other activities that were going on. In addition, we had the financial resources from both the university and the federal government to carry out our activities. My approach was to build programs with a strong foundation that would be lasting, and that would serve a significant component of the undergraduate minority and handicapper population enrolling at MSU. This is where I put my energy.

My approach was not always understood and appreciated by the staff working in support of the disadvantaged. Part of the problem, if there was one, was that as a chemist/scientist I was very objective and data oriented by habit, while staff members were counselors with a human concern for students, and with less obligation to objectivity and data. This would plague us for some time, until the U.S. Department of Education began to press for more and more data. Then I was redeemed in the eyes of the staff.

In the early stages there was the Center for Supportive Services and the Special Services for the Disadvantaged Students Program (SSDSP). From the outset there was a fair amount of confusion about the target population of each. The center focused on Developmental Program students, while SSDSP served low-income students irrespective of racial/ethnic background. The faculty presumably believed that we were in business to serve all minority students, as they saw all minority students with the exception of Asian Americans as disadvantaged. Moreover, it seemed to me the faculty tended to equate minority with African American. So we were constantly being construed as an African American student program rather than a program for the disadvantaged. Actually, our target populations were reasonably well defined. Confusion entered the picture because the university was not able to identify for us those students who were low income. That was not information sought during the admissions process. When we did get such data from the Office of Financial Aids, there was substantial overlap between the low-income students and those admitted through the Developmental Program. Further confounding matters was the fact that in both groups almost all of the students identified as low income were African American, so that we were by and large an African American program. We just did not serve all the African Americans enrolling at the university. This would be a matter of some confusion throughout the life of the program.

The Office of Special Programs suffered from two problems. One was the lack of adequate organizational structure, and the other was the lack of sufficient space in one location for all the units. The Center for Supportive Services was in the Union Building, SSDSP was in Holden Hall, and the handicapper program was in the Library. Moreover, the leadership of the Center for Supportive Services had changed when Henry Johnson completed his Ph.D. and moved on to the East Coast. His replacement was Laura Henderson, whose background was in counseling and who seemed to be the right person for the job. I appointed her assistant director of special programs and hired Florence Harris, who had worked as an academic intern in the Center for Supportive Services, to coordinate the center. Henry Braddock continued as associate director of the federally funded SSDSP. It soon became clear that trying to run the operation with three different locations was difficult. In addition, we were operating two tutorial programs, one in the Center for Supportive Services and another in special programs. There was a need to bring the staffs together so that they could communicate more effectively. In addition, the assistant and associate directors had overlapping responsibilities. The opportunity arose to deal with this problem when Henry Braddock was called up to the military and sent to Panama. I immediately took steps to merge the Special Services Program with the Center for Supportive Services, but I was not able to put them in common space at this time.

I put the administrative staff in the Union Building in space occupied by the Center for Supportive Services and put all the specialists in Holden Hall. The handicapper student program was assigned its own assistant director. I assumed responsibility as assistant provost and director of special programs. My purposes were clear; I wanted to merge all the programs, put them under a more central administration, and delegate some of the responsibility. I had in mind, as I informed the staff, that eventually I wanted to name a new director for the program. All of this tended to cause confusion and fostered a sense of uncertainty and insecurity among the staff. I wrote about this extensively in a report on special programs covering the 1974-75 academic year. The staff reacted to these changes, as well as to the classification shift mentioned earlier (from Administrative Professional to Specialist). There was also frustration among assistant directors in the old structure, who wanted more independence and authority to manage the programs. Frankly, at the time I could not confidently delegate that responsibility to any of the people in those positions and preferred retaining control. Good or bad, that was the decision I made and the one I functioned under for the rest of this period.

Assistant Director Laura Henderson, an African American, developed a rebuttal to my annual report for the 1975 academic year. It was an absolute shock to me. I had thought that we had a working relationship within which that kind of thing would not occur. Her report suggested to me that she had feelings and concerns about her role in Special Programs and her relationship to me that she had been holding in. Although Henderson had a right to submit her report internally, she took the added step of providing a copy to the program officer in the U.S. Department of Education. without consulting me, the program director and assistant provost, or anyone else in the Provost's Office; in my opinion, by doing so, she jeopardized MSU's funding support. My reaction was to discontinue her from her position forthwith, along with Penny Adkins in the Office of Programs for Handicapper Students and Bertram Green and Sylvia Jackson within the Special Services Program. This led to a grievance being filed against me under the faculty grievance system at Michigan State University.

Dealing with grievances was unfamiliar territory. The hearing had a negative effect on me, and I think it contributed to the fact that I was soon diagnosed as having high blood pressure. The faculty grievance officer at the time was Bruce Miller, a professor of philosophy. Laura Henderson had counsel in the person of attorney Zolton Ferency, a professor in the School of Criminal Justice, noted for adopting liberal causes within the institution. I made a serious error that I would never repeat: I decided to represent myself in the hearings. This was very difficult for me to deal with, and it took its toll physically and emotionally. The outcome was that the plaintiff was granted a temporary assignment in another unit within the university. She and her family eventually moved from the area after she resigned her position at MSU.

By now I wanted out and was looking around for other things to do. There was a change in leadership in the Office of the Provost with the appointment of Lawrence Boger as provost, formerly dean of the College of Agriculture and Natural Resources. Lee Winder at that time was associate provost, and both were in position when the controversy arose in special programs during the 1975-76 academic year. In 1976 the provost appointed a committee to review special programs. The committee interviewed all the staff in the units that reported to me and spent a considerable amount of time with me as well. The committee recommended appointment of a director of special programs who would have major responsibility for all decisions within the program and who would report to the provost through the assistant provost for special programs. Staff had expressed concern about too much data being collected, but the committee recommended that even more be gathered about what the programs were achieving within MSU. They recommended that the Office of Programs for Handicapped Students be physically separated from special programs and reassigned under the vice president for student affairs and services. The committee further proposed placement of the transportation program for handicappers under automotive services or the campus bus system. Neither of these two recommendations was adopted. The provost did appoint a search and select committee for the new director of special programs, and I served on that body.

Ultimately, Provost Boger appointed Dr. Christine Wilson, an African American, as director. Dr. Wilson reported to the assistant provost for special programs. I gave her free rein to coordinate the merged Special Services Program, the Center for Supportive Services, and Upward Bound. The handicapper component was assigned its own director, who continued to report directly to the assistant provost. In 1976-77, I moved on to assume responsibilities as both assistant dean of the Graduate School and assistant provost for special programs.

▼

CHAPTER FIVE

MORE ADMINISTERING, FAMILY, & MAEOPP 1976-1979

M y appointment in the Graduate School was fortuitous. The entire graduate area had been reorganized following the resignation of Milton Muelder, the vice president for research and advanced graduate studies. Rumor had it that he had served in the military in World War II and was present in an official capacity during the Nuremberg Trials. President Wharton then appointed John Cantlon as vice president for research and graduate studies. It was at this same time that Lawrence Boger, former dean of agriculture, became provost at Michigan State University, although he would leave that post in less than a year to become president of Oklahoma State. Cantlon established a separate office and position for dean of the Graduate School and appointed Herbert Oyer, a professor of audiology and speech sciences, to be dean. Oyer undertook a search for a new assistant dean, whose responsibilities would include management of the university's EOP Fellowship Program for minority graduate students. This program, established within the Center for Urban Affairs in the early 1970s, had been administered by that unit for the first few years and then transferred to the Graduate School.

I moved into this position happily, not at all aware of what it would be like to divide my time among the Graduate School, Special Programs, and chemistry, where I still taught and had graduate students. I welcomed the change. Effective July 1, 1976, I became assistant dean of the Graduate School on a half-time basis, and my responsibilities included the EOP Fellowship Program; the Committee on Institutional Cooperation (CIC), the Big Ten schools plus the University of Chicago; Traveling Scholars Program; Michigan Intercollegiate Graduate Studies Program; and liaison with the National Science Foundation's Fellowship Programs. I also served on the Graduate Assistant Dean's Group and on the Affirmative Action Graduate Assistantship Committee. One major accomplishment during my stay was to resist the division of the EOP Fellowship Program into components for medical school students, urban counseling students, and others. Another major accomplishment was to assist Dean Oyer in developing a new minority competitive doctoral fellowship program.

I particularly enjoyed representing the Graduate School at meetings of the Council of Graduate Schools and the Association of Graduate Schools. There I had the opportunity to meet other individuals with whom I would have significant interaction in the years ahead. One was the vice provost for minority affairs at Ohio State University, who at the time was assistant dean of the Graduate School there. Another was Shirley Malcolm, an African American who worked at the American Association for the Advancement of Science in Washington, D.C., where she aggressively pushed to increase the numbers of African Americans, Hispanics, Native Americans, and handicappers who went on to graduate study in the sciences. Shirley McBay, another African American, was a program officer in the Office of Minority Opportunities at the National Science Foundation in Washington, D.C.

While I enjoyed my duties in the Graduate School, in the final analysis I could not divide myself three ways for more than a year. I relinquished my position and returned to full-time duties as assistant provost for special programs. By now I had been appointed associate professor of chemistry.

It was not all work and no play in those days. I regularly played a "nickel, dime, quarter" poker game with Les Rout and a number of his peers from the Department of History or related areas. Bob Fiore, a professor in the Department of Romance Languages, joined the game later. We had a lot of fun. No one lost much money. The organizer was invariably Les Rout, a specialist in Latin

American studies and fluent in Spanish and Portuguese, who did extensive research on African Americans in Latin America. Poker was relaxation for all of us.

▼   ▼   ▼

Meanwhile, my children were growing up. They were making their impact felt in many ways around the house. With my son I did all the things a father typically does, including some that fathers did not do, at least when I was a child. For example, when Bramlett was about four years old, an Indian Guide group was formed in the community. Typically, mothers led the group in this period of heightened consciousness and the push for increased access and rights for women. But I became the head advisor to the Indian Guides, who met regularly to talk about Indian lore. (Later, Bramlett moved on to the Cub Scouts, and I became the "den mother" as well.) In 1972, he began kindergarten at Wardcliff Elementary School. We felt very fortunate that Bramlett went to that school because there was an African American principal, Jeff Richburg. Jeff was also an avid chess player. By the time Bramlett entered elementary school he had already learned the rudiments of chess, and he received more reinforcement from the principal. I still remember him going off to school on that first day, which he wanted to do alone. I see him now, turning that last corner and going out of sight.

Priscilla Lamisi was then going on two. She had spoken her first word at Disneyland, which we visited in summer 1972. That word was "look"—an appropriate word at a place like Disneyland in California. Priscilla began kindergarten at Wardcliff in 1976, but after our move to Shaker Heights in Okemos, Michigan, the next year, she and Bramlett transferred to Edgewood Elementary, right behind our house. Ruth and I were very active in the Wardcliff and Edgewood parent groups and in other ways, volunteering for different activities. We had both learned, and Ruth more than I, that parents need to be very supportive of their children when they go to school, and we dedicated ourselves to that.

It was when Bramlett joined the Cub Scouts that I began baking 7-Up pound cakes, on my own no less. Every year the Cub Scouts held a father and son cake bake, and we had to bake, decorate, and compete for prizes. We did not win the first year, but we definitely won the second year with a cake decorated to represent a camp site for Cub Scouts. I used dyed green coconut for the grass and pretzel sticks for the picket fences.

Ruth worked with Priscilla in the Brownies and later with the Girl Scouts. Priscilla stayed with this for a while but soon grew tired of it. She was a much more independent child than her brother. He was very outgoing, and both had enjoyed the benefit of lots of company around the house as children. There was never a dull moment in the Hamilton household when Bramlett and Priscilla were young, with the various African American and African students who saw us as a second home. We encouraged students to come by anytime, and they did. We read to the children a great deal, and I can recall making up stories for Priscilla at night. She encouraged me in this, and I liked to do it. It had been done for me as a child as well.

Our children had a very different upbringing from their father. For example, they went to schools that were predominantly white. There were a few African Americans and many more Asian students in their school, but by and large minorities were isolated as a group and individually. My daughter recently told me about a fight she had when a white student used the term "nigger" in class. I also recall a young child referring to Bramlett as a "nigger" as they passed our house on the way to elementary school. Ruth happened to hear it, and the next day she stopped the child on his way to school and talked to him about it. She told him she knew his parents, that he had learned better at home, and that he should refer to Bramlett by his name in the future. The very next day the young man brought Ruth some wild flowers that he pulled somewhere along the roadside and apologized.

My son at the age of four had traveled to London and to Africa, in contrast to his father, who had never left the country until he joined the Marine Corps. Similarly, my daughter had traveled extensively by the time she reached her teen years. She went to

Egypt and Kenya with her mother and later with her mother and me to England, France, and Italy. Our son went as an exchange student to Bogota, Colombia, and later studied in Spain and at Cambridge in England, and traveled to other areas in Europe. We made it a point of taking vacations, usually at different places, when the children were young. We made the usual stops at Disneyland, Disneyworld, and Washington, D.C. We were avid campers, largely due to my insistence, and went camping everywhere in Michigan.

The children had early training in music. Ruth saw to that. Each of them participated in the Suzuki piano program, taking lessons from Dorothy Rubin, an Okemos instructor who taught by this method. This was an excellent exposure that began early for both of the children. I believe that by the age of six each of them was studying piano. Priscilla would stay with piano much longer than did our son, who switched to the alto saxophone when he went to middle school. Priscilla also played first chair oboe in the high school band. Both were in their school band and orchestra, and both received excellent musical instruction from outstanding professors at Michigan State University. Priscilla remains a very good pianist, having studied with Professor Deborah Moriarity of MSU's School of Music for seven years. Likewise, Bramlett was a longtime student of James Forger, saxophonist and current head of the School of Music at MSU. Being active musically was great for the kids educationally and socially. The Okemos School District gave great emphasis to music. Through music the children met a number of young people with whom they continue to remain close.

Ruth and I were always concerned that the children understand just how important their education was. This meant providing a lot of support to them throughout their schooling. Of course, they had the big advantage of having two academic parents, although I am sure this also put undue pressure on them. They were not unlike many other students in the Okemos School District who came from relatively advantaged backgrounds.

Our children finally made the trek to Yellowstone National Park and Grand Teton National Park with us in 1977. Bramlett was ten years old, and Priscilla was six. On the way, we stopped in Ames to visit with old friends and see Mary Greeley Hospital, where Bramlett had been born. We took our tent with us and did some camping en route.

Once on the open road, across the Mississippi going west, not many thoughts of your job or other worries and concerns enter into your mind. You enter another world, and you are surrounded by vacationers on the highways. When we went on that trip I had not overcome my fear of heights and continued to have concerns about the mountains as we approached. The first big group was the Black Hills of South Dakota. We had stopped earlier at the Badlands and run around in those crusty areas for a while, on into the evening. We then made the late drive on to the Black Hills and Custer State Park. We had difficulty finding it. Ruth was driving, fortunately, for we ended up on the Needles Highway pretty far up, certainly well above 8,000 or 9,000 feet, driving on one-lane roads through many tunnels and looking up at needle-like rock formations. I can remember that my daughter's reaction to all this was to go to sleep immediately. We were all tired, especially Ruth, when we finally reached Custer State Park, raised our tent, and settled down for the evening.

The next day we had an opportunity to see a buffalo herd. We again made the obligatory trip to Mount Rushmore to see the sculptures of the presidents. Then it was on to Wyoming and the Big Horn Mountain Range, which I would drive through again, with Ruth's assistance. Yellowstone was even more impressive to me on the second trip. My fear of heights had grown, and the children made me nervous everywhere we went in the park. I can remember them standing close to the edge of Yellowstone Canyon looking over at the falls, and how nervous that made me. Nonetheless, they were as thrilled as we always knew our children would be with Yellowstone National Park.

We then went south to Grand Teton National Park, which was our favorite, where we stayed in Coulter Bay Cabins and forgot about tent life for a while. This was very comfortable. In the Tetons we did everything you could do. We took the raft trip down the Snake River, and we went hiking virtually every day into the Tetons. We went to Jackson Hole and ate and shopped. My son and

I went fishing on the Snake River, and he caught a sizable cutthroat trout. Bramlett started reeling in the fish and then, in his excitement, dropped the pole, ran into the water, and literally grabbed the fish and carried it out! Bystanders gathered, they were all so happy for him. He caught two more fish before he was through. We took them to the Coulter Bay Cabins Restaurant, and, would you believe it, the chef prepared them in a most delicious manner and served them to us himself at breakfast the next day. It was quite a memorable occasion for me, the proud father, and for Bramlett, the young fisherman.

Overall, our stay in the Tetons and in Yellowstone had been all that we had thought it would be many years earlier. We returned home well rested and full of memories of an exciting journey.

▼   ▼   ▼

The following four events changed forever the relationship of the U.S. Congress to TRIO programs and to the Mid-America Association of Educational Opportunity Program Personnel (MAEOPP). Below, each of these and its effect are described in some detail.

1. The formation of the Mid-America Association of Educational Opportunity Program Personnel (MAEOPP).
2. A visit to Washington, D.C., bureaucrats and to legislators by MAEOPP representatives, including: its president, Rozelle Boyd; its executive director, Arnold Mitchem; and members of the Board of Directors, Joe Lewis, of Central State University in Ohio, and me.
3. A letter from me to the chairman of the U.S. Committee on Postsecondary Education of the U.S. House, Representative James O'Hara, that led to a major change in the relationship of MAEOPP to the Washington scene.
4. The presentation of testimony by me and Arnold Mitchem before Representative O'Hara's committee in the U.S. House of Representatives in Washington, D.C.

MAEOPP was established in 1974 at The Abbey in Lake Fontana, Wisconsin. I was present on that historic occasion, as were many, many others. The association chose Arnold Mitchem as executive director. An election for president was to be held, and Rozelle Boyd had declared his candidacy. Clark Chipman and Clara Fitzpatrick encouraged me to run, and Manuel Pierson of Oakland University volunteered to be my campaign manager. Still, I was reluctant for several reasons. First, I believed that Rozelle, who was very well known throughout the region and had arrived on the TRIO scene earlier than I, would win. Second, Rozelle Boyd was an experienced politician, an elected representative on the Democratic ticket of the Indianapolis, Indiana, City Council. Rozelle had the wherewithal to function politically, as the first president of this organization must. Third, I was an academician and still saw myself in that way. While I was involved with MAEOPP and with TRIO programs, at this time, 1974-75, I had not made a full and long-term commitment and did not wish to entangle myself by becoming president of the body. I also felt that with my background I did not fit. What I did not know was how much the association, the people within it, and the mission they had adopted would become a part of the rest of my life. In retrospect, I might have made a different decision and run a stronger race, but I still might have lost. Needless to say, Rozelle, my dear friend, won and served as president for two years.

I also believe that I was pressed to run because there was a residual fear, among some members, of Arnold Mitchem's leadership style. Arnold is an astute politician and, like many astute politicians, he does not always do what "you" want. Some in MAEOPP incorrectly saw me as a better balance to Arnold than was Boyd. I am convinced that throughout his leadership of the association, which continues to the present, Arnold has sought to meet the needs of the membership, the association at large, and TRIO programs. He has, indeed, excelled in this capacity. I also believe that I made major contributions to both the Region V TRIO Advisory Council and to all the discussions that ultimately led to the creation of a regional association. In addition, I contributed later in other ways, such as presenting testimony to the U.S. House

Subcommittee on Post-Secondary Education. Over the years, I became known as a major advocate for evaluation of support programs. The new association called on me to do workshops at different places around the country. It had always been my expectation that the association would design model support programs that would be adopted by universities and colleges across the nation. MAEOPP would later develop models, but these would not be widely adopted. On the contrary, most universities and colleges proceeded to develop additional support programs independent of any TRIO program existing on their campuses.

MSU was probably typical. Here we saw the emergence, even as early as 1968, of support programs in colleges operating with support of the faculty. That pattern would be repeated in several colleges at MSU, including the Colleges of Business, Engineering, and Natural Science. They, too, brought in academic paraprofessionals to run the programs, but the programs existed with the full knowledge and support of the faculty. Even today, TRIO programs exist on campuses independent of the mainstream, although there are exceptions. MSU is one of those that endeavors to involve the faculty in its TRIO activities, yet TRIO does not have an academic home in a college or department at MSU and does not enjoy broadly based faculty support or faculty awareness of its existence.

Under the leadership of Arnold Mitchem, MAEOPP placed greater emphasis upon increasing federal funding for the TRIO programs and on training and development of staff. MAEOPP's goal was advocacy for low-income and disadvantaged students at the national level and the identification and protection of the federal resources that had been appropriated and allocated for TRIO programs. (The programs are: Talent Search, for identifying low-income youth with the potential for higher education, and then orienting them and assisting them in applying for admission to colleges and universities; Upward Bound, which has a summer and an academic year component for low-income and first-generation students, providing them with the basic skills and motivation to enroll in higher education; and Special Services for Disadvantaged Students Programs, to provide low-income students enrolled in higher education with academic support services, such as counseling, tutoring, and basic skills development, to help them realize academic success.)

In addition, MAEOPP sought to provide workshops and training for its professional members in annual conferences. I have noted one of the first positions created was that of executive director, whose job it was to work the Washington scene on behalf of the association and its members. MAEOPP and the executive director became the newest and one of the more effective lobbies for programs that have a major effect on minority access to and retention in higher education institutions. It became a parallel group to the National Association for Equal Opportunity (NAFEO), which is an organization of HBCU presidents that also maintains a lobbyist in Washington.

I joined with Arnold Mitchem, Rozelle Boyd, and Joe Lewis on a trip to Washington, where we hoped to make an impact on those responsible for TRIO in the U.S. Office of Education, on members of the U.S. House of Representatives, or on staff at the executive level. This was a bold venture for us, since rarely had program personnel made their presences felt in the Capitol. We began at the program officer level, which at that time included such individuals as David Johnson and Leonard Spearman (who was the overall director of the division). All these people told us to go back home. They advised us they had things well in hand and could take care of the legislation, the authorizations, and the appropriations discussions in the House of Representatives and elsewhere. They really discouraged us.

We then went to a higher level within the U.S. Office of Education. There we met with a couple of deputy directors who were more receptive to our visit. I can recall that one of them in particular wished to discuss an evaluation model for Special Services Programs, and he presented in detail an approach that was under consideration and would subsequently be implemented. These government officials also had much nicer offices than did the program officers and the director of our division, who were, relatively speaking, housed in slum-like conditions.

From the department we went for an appointment with U.S. Commissioner of the Office of Education Terrance Bell. We waited and waited, but it was clear that we would have difficulty seeing the commissioner and making the rest of our appointments. Therefore, we left Bell's office, leaving our regrets, and proceeded to a different experience with the Office of Management and Budget. It seemed an appropriate place to go, since it was here that priorities of the administration were set. This meeting began badly. For example, all of us were seated on a relatively low couch, while the official with whom we met sat in a significantly higher chair, enabling him to look down on us. He kept control of the meeting throughout and lectured us about the need for training our personnel in the field. We seldom got to the points that we wanted to raise, and when we did our host managed to avoid giving definitive responses. From the Office of Management and Budget we proceeded to the U.S. House of Representatives.

There we hoped to meet with the chair of the House Subcommittee on Postsecondary Education, Rep. William O'Hara of Michigan. We were welcomed with open arms by his aide, James Harrison, who was especially glad to see people from the field who were knowledgeable about TRIO programs. We had a good discussion with Mr. Harrison. Arnold Mitchem led the way or, as he often did, listened, observed, and considered the right point at which to introduce the key comments or questions that he wanted to make. This was our best meeting of all.

At the end of each of the three days we would return to our hotel and consider what we had achieved and learned during that day's visit. We left Washington feeling that we had accomplished our goal. We returned to our respective institutions and later gave reports on the trip to the TRIO Programs Advisory Council.

In 1975 the U.S. House of Representatives through Representative William O'Hara announced hearings on the TRIO programs. I did not think about the implications for MAEOPP at the time, but I did think about the implications for Michigan State University. I sat down at my desk and dictated a letter to Representative O'Hara expressing interest in testifying before his committee. I was pleased shortly thereafter to receive an invitation. When the news of my appearance circulated, I heard from a number of people regarding my testimony and what it might be. I received a rather interesting letter from Arnold Mitchem, cautioning me that I was not a spokesperson for MAEOPP. A similar letter, I am sure, went from him to Representative O'Hara, who wrote advising me that others would be testifying at the hearings, including Arnold Mitchem, Dot Ruth (an advisor/consultant to Leonard Spearman, head of the Division of Student Support Services), and Glen Ellis, who was also heading an educational opportunity program.

I proceeded to develop my detailed testimony. I shared the draft with Clark Chipman, with the executive board of MAEOPP, and with Leonard Spearman and Dave Johnson in the U.S. Office of Education. I received useful suggestions from several people and incorporated those into my testimony, which I delivered before the subcommittee on April 11, 1975. Needless to say, I was quite nervous about the whole thing. Nonetheless, I read my testimony on that historic day. I was the only person to make a point of how much the authorization and appropriation levels for these programs should become in the next fiscal year. I referred to a figure of $250 million. The 1975 appropriation was $70 million. I can distinctly remember Representative O'Hara raising his head and staring at me following my reference to a quarter of a billion dollars. The hearings were a historic occasion for TRIO and for MAEOPP. I had stumbled in and triggered a series of events that would reverberate for decades across the nation and in the Capitol. Following the presentation of all the testimony, James Harrison invited those who had testified to meet with him immediately. He asked us to draft the legislation and send it to him. Never again would TRIO programs and related legislation be moved forward without consultation with MAEOPP.

I continued to be an active member of the association, and I served one year as program chair of the annual conference. This was another historic occasion, when Representative Shirley Chisolm appeared before the association. MAEOPP has continued the strong traditions begun earlier of active involvement in the political process, and this has served the association well. It has not been so strong programmatically, in the sense of having a major effect in determining the direction of EOP or academic support programs within higher education institutions across the country.

Perhaps that was too much to expect, although some of us in the earlier days certainly saw the association as being in a position to have significant influence in this area as well.

▼   ▼   ▼

At Michigan State, on November 15, 1976, we entered a new era during which Dr. Christine Wilson served as director of Support Services. She was formerly director of women's programs, so she had experience in administration, albeit not with a program for providing academic support to undergraduates. She had the advantage of having all support services in one area of campus. The program at this time consisted of the institutionally funded program that was formerly the Center for Supportive Services and the federally funded Special Services for Disadvantaged Students Program. These two were merged, since all along we had been using the institutionally funded component for matching federal funds under the federal grant. In addition, the Upward Bound program, formerly directed by Alex Cade, was included. A professor in the College of Education, Alex had been the original project director for Upward Bound and had developed the first successful proposal for funding. The problem Alex had was that the environment for TRIO programs had changed. There was a new group of paraprofessionals in Michigan, across the Midwest, and nationally who were successfully writing proposals and getting funding. Alex and his staff were unwilling to interact with this new group, which lacked academic credentials. The Upward Bound program needed new leadership, and I had appointed Keith Williams, an African American who had taught in the program for several years, as director. The entire supportive services staff was located in East Holden Hall in the academic wing. Florence Harris, who had been a coordinator for the Center for Supportive Services, was assigned responsibilities as assistant to the director. All of this provided a real opportunity for the program to move ahead in a systematic way.

Supportive services had always operated using both a decentralized and a centralized model. We offered assistance through departments as well as directly through the unit. Christine Wilson had the additional charge to continue "providing funding to stimulate the development of decentralized supportive services." Included among some of these were programs in the departments of Chemistry, Mathematics, and American Thought and Language, the Learning Resources Center, and the College of Natural Science. In addition, some funding was being channeled to the Career Resources Center under the vice president for student affairs and services. This decentralized versus centralized approach had also been a bone of contention between me and the administrative staff.

The emphasis upon gathering systematic data on the results of program implementation was retained, as this had been a firm recommendation of the review committee. The program moved ahead. The staff had great expectations, as they now had the independence they had sought!

The Office of Programs for Handicapper Students under Judy Taylor continued to report centrally to the assistant provost. That program was on firm ground and had a clear mission with relatively little, if any, ambiguity. The major concern at this time was how it would expand the commitment of services to the deaf student population, who presented particular challenges.

During this period I carried dual responsibilities as assistant provost for special programs and as assistant dean of the Graduate School. In spite of that, I saw the opportunity to begin some new initiatives and mounted a new publication in the university, *The Bulletin, Office of Special Programs*. This newsletter was published twice a year and became a vehicle for communicating to the rest of the university and our students what was happening in the units reporting to the assistant provost for special programs. The first volume gave particular emphasis to Christine Wilson and her staff.

Meanwhile, many changes were taking place at MSU under the provost. When Larry Boger accepted the presidency of Oklahoma State University, Associate Provost Lee Winder became acting provost and then provost in 1976. Dr. Jack B. Kinsinger, then chair of the Department of Chemistry, became the associate provost. It was Jack who had hired me into the department in 1969. We were about to begin a new era together in the Office of the Provost. We were also beginning a period of budget uncertainties as a university in the state of Michigan.

There were also major problems with intercollegiate athletics. We were investigated by the NCAA, and our football program was placed on probation. This was a traumatic time for MSU. Duffy Daugherty had retired as football coach a year or two earlier. His replacement, Denny Stolz, would soon leave MSU for Bowling Green State University in Ohio.

In 1977 President Wharton accepted the position of chancellor of the state of New York's university system. I was very sorry to see him leave MSU. He came to MSU during the period of campus protest against the Vietnam War. Demonstrations were common, and at one point state police in helmets and with nightsticks had to be called in to control rampaging students. There was even a time when students constructed what came to be called "Tent City" in the area behind Erickson Hall. But the biggest disruption occurred when students blocked Grand River Avenue in front of the Union Building, and police were forced to use tear gas to clear the area. The tear gas seeped into the Union Building and even into Cowles House, where the president lived. Throughout all this, President Wharton and his wife, Dolores, remained accessible to students and often met with them on the steps of their home. When African American students expressed concerns about the antiwar demonstrations and declared a "zone of liberation" to discuss their concerns, President Wharton and several others made presentations to a group of African American administrators, faculty, and students in Wells Hall. The president managed to lead MSU through the antiwar period without the major damage that struck other campuses, such as the University of Wisconsin-Madison.

Clifton and Dolores Wharton were a new experience for MSU and the greater Lansing community, with which they both became familiar. President Wharton, an easterner and former advisor to Nelson Rockefeller, gave MSU renewed visibility on a national level, both because he was the first African American president of a large, predominantly white university and because of his connections with eastern elites. The Whartons accomplished a great deal at Michigan State. Deeply interested in the fine arts, they spearheaded

a major fund-raising campaign for the construction of a new performing arts center at MSU that later bore their name. The kickoff
was at Munn Ice Arena and brought Lena Horne and Tony Bennett
to campus.

During President Wharton's tenure the number of African
American and Hispanic students at MSU rose significantly. In
addition, the expansion of Wells Hall was completed and became
the new home of the Department of Mathematics. There were
changes at the administrative level as well. The president appointed
Lloyd Cofer, an African American, as his assistant. He also named a
new vice president for student affairs and services, Eldon
Nonnamaker; a new provost; and a new vice president for research
and graduate studies. The president had intended to appoint an
African American male to the student affairs position, but at the
last minute the person accepted a position as president of a community college district. I came to know President Wharton very
well. His office was always open, and I felt that I could drop in to
see him at any time, although I never abused that option.

President Wharton never had the full support of the Board of
Trustees; he came to MSU with a five-to-three vote. (One board
member who favored Wharton's appointment was Don Stevens,
who lost his job and the backing of his party because of it. There
were rumors that unions in Michigan wanted Don to support former Governor G. Mennen Williams as a candidate.) Despite the
close vote, during his eight years President Wharton accomplished
a great deal, including setting MSU in a new direction related to
admission of undergraduate, graduate, and graduate/professional
students. He was the first president to commit MSU to greater
access for handicapper and disadvantaged students as well as students from minority backgrounds, the older student, and the lifelong student. He appointed a task force to report on lifelong
learning and the role of MSU in this regard. Although that program did not bear fruit during his stay, the results of broadened
access are reflected throughout this book. President Wharton benefited in part from the better financial circumstances for MSU than
would be the case in later years, although we could see the beginning of financial problems even then.

As noted earlier, the Whartons were accessible to African American and other students at MSU, and they were frequently observed in the audience when major visitors came to campus. During the Wharton years, honorary degrees were granted to Walter Cronkite and to Dr. Percy Julian (the first African American to be admitted to the U.S. Academy of Sciences). Dolores Wharton made a point of being present when Minister Farrakhan spoke at Michigan State in the early 1970s. He would later visit the campus under greater controversy.

At the opening ceremony for the Clifton and Dolores Wharton Center for the Performing Arts, I have never seen such a warm and thunderous reception as they received. They loved and were great supporters of our university, and they cherish their many friends and associates at MSU. President Wharton left MSU to become chancellor of the largest university system in the United States, and from there he moved on to become chairman and chief operating officer of TIAA-CREF, one of the largest retirement programs in the world. More recently, his career in public service reached a new peak with his appointment as assistant secretary of state by President Clinton.

▼   ▼   ▼

Not long after Christine Wilson assumed her responsibilities, I took her around the state and the nation to introduce her to people she needed to know in various professional organizations and in the U.S. Department of Education. For example, she met the members of MAEOPP, at the annual conference in Fontana, Wisconsin, and Clark Chipman, who was still the region's program officer in the U.S. Department of Education. Dr. Wilson served as director of Supportive Services until she resigned her position and eventually left MSU in July 1979. Her formal assignment as a staff member and assistant professor in special programs ended in March of that year. I then appointed Florence Harris, who had been with the program since 1971. The program has continued to grow, prosper, and expand under her leadership.

I recommended to the provost at the end of 1978 that a committee be established to review campus services for students from minority and disadvantaged backgrounds. The provost agreed, and a group was formed in January 1979; at my recommendation, it was chaired by Dr. Lee June, then of the Counseling Center. The committee included representatives from the provost area who were involved in support services as well as representatives from the office of the vice president for student affairs and services. In addition, there were faculty representatives and delegates from various racial/ethnic groups on campus. I served in an ex-officio capacity, along with several others, and provided support to the committee in various forms throughout its deliberations. The charge to the committee was as follows:

1. Inventory the services now provided and the units involved.
2. Make an assessment, insofar as possible, of the extent to which the services are meeting the needs of students.
3. Review relationships among the Office of Supportive Services, the Learning Resources Center, and other support programs and activities.
4. Recommend ways to improve communication and coordination among the various units involved in managing support services for disadvantaged and minority students.
5. Recommend ways to divide responsibilities so that resources will be used as effectively and efficiently as possible.
6. Review institutional policies and practices as they operate to implement or hinder the academic progress of minority and disadvantaged students. Develop recommendations for consideration, as deemed necessary.
7. Recommend a mechanism or mechanisms for the development of recommendations for changes in policy and practices to university administrators and governance groups.

In short, the committee was grappling with an old issue that had plagued the Office of Special Programs for almost a decade: how to serve the disadvantaged, who were largely minority, and yet not overlook the needs of other minorities, who may not be disadvantaged.

The committee of about 15 met over the next six months, and the final report was completed and presented to the provost in July 1979. The first recommendations ranged from admissions and financial aid, to the role of the Office of Supportive Services and the Office of the Assistant Provost for Special Programs, to new mechanisms university-wide for achieving greater coordination of support services. For example, it was proposed that a new unit be established to coordinate the admission of minority students and to monitor the admission of each racial/ethnic group. This had always been done for students admitted under the Developmental Program, but it was proposed that this be done more comprehensively for all minority students. It was recommended that there be new scholarships for talented minority students, and that these funds be renewable for these students, based upon academic performance, for up to four years.

The committee expressed concerns about the Developmental Program; its very name seemed demeaning and inappropriate. Accordingly, it was changed to College Achievement Admission Program. The committee also recommended that the Office of Supportive Services be changed to College Achievement Program. The report went on to suggest that funds be made available to establish a summer admissions program for all minority students and/or College Achievement Admission Program students. In the summer, over ten weeks, these students would get an extended orientation to university life and have an opportunity to strengthen basic skills in writing, reading, and mathematics. It also was recommended that the assistant provost have a broader role in seeking external funding for minority student support. To facilitate this, it was proposed that his administrative secretary become an administrative assistant and that he get a new secretary.

These were new and fascinating proposals for Michigan State University. For the first time we saw some clear thinking about how MSU could move forward to improve the admission of minority and disadvantaged students and improve their retention. For example, the report proposed that the university change the charge to the Office of Supportive Services so that it served minority students as well as students admitted under the Developmental

Program for Admissions. It was also urged that adequate resources be provided to carry out that new charge.

The various colleges were not told to establish new support programs, but they were urged to take a greater interest in the retention of all undergraduates, to be prepared to report on the retention of minority undergraduate students enrolled in their programs, and to be prepared to work in a mutually supportive manner with other groups on campus, such as the Office of Supportive Services.

Finally, the report proposed that the vice president for student affairs establish the position of director, dean, or assistant vice president for minority programs who would function as a liaison with the Office of Supportive Services and other support programs on campus, and who would work with minority undergraduates and residence hall programs serving these students. It also was proposed that the equivalent of a Supportive Services Advisory Committee be established and charged with bringing together personnel across the university involved with support programs, so that they could coordinate their activities and function in an advisory way to the Office of the Provost.

This was new stuff! The committee had fulfilled its charge. Lee June and all the members had pointed down a new path for the university, and it was now up to the provost to determine which of these recommendations, if any, were to become reality.

In the same year, 1979, I was invited to join a National Science Foundation team that would be visiting several institutions (Atlanta University Center, University of Texas at San Antonio, University of New Mexico at Albuquerque, and New Mexico State University) to determine which should receive National Science Foundation grants to establish regional centers for minorities in science and engineering. These comprehensive centers were to function from precollege to university level.

Then, in 1979, I was approached by the deputy director for research at Argonne National Laboratory, who inquired about my interest in becoming director of their Division of Educational Programs. Needless to say, I was surprised and pleased to have been sought out. Over the next few weeks, I learned considerably more about this position and accepted it for one year. Lee June acted as assistant provost for special programs in my absence. One of my last acts before leaving for Argonne was to meet with the MSU Board of Trustees to present the report of the Ad Hoc Committee on Supportive Services for Minority Students and Students from Disadvantaged Backgrounds. President Cecil Mackey replaced Edgar Harden as president of Michigan State, Harden having served in the interim after President Wharton's departure.

▼

CHAPTER SIX

A LEAVE AT ARGONNE
NATIONAL LABORATORY

Argonne was a totally new and different experience. To this
day, I do not know who put Mike Nevitt, deputy director
for research, on my trail. He offered me the job after my
first visit to the laboratory in May 1979. As director of the Division
of Educational Programs, I would be one of a number of senior
staff within the laboratory, all of whom were running research
divisions. My assignment was to handle educational programs and
to monitor relationships between the laboratory and the universities in the Argonne Universities Association, to which the laboratory was partly responsible at that time. The association included
most of the major research institutions of the AAU type in the
Midwest. Argonne had a number of facilities used by scientists and
engineers in the universities, and the association, together with the
University of Chicago, was part of the governance structure for the
laboratory. My specific responsibilities covered two key programs.

1. Under the auspices of the International Atomic Energy Agency
   in Vienna, Austria, nuclear power project training courses were
   offered to less-developed countries considering nuclear reactors
   as an alternative energy resource. (This was 1979, before
   Chernoble but after Three Mile Island.)
2. An undergraduate research participation program operated during the summer as well as the academic year. Among all the
   national laboratories responsible to the U.S. Department of

Energy, Argonne had the largest program of this kind in the country. The division served essentially honors students and was very selective. The students had an opportunity to work with some of the top scientists and engineers in the nation, and on some of the most exciting research projects.

In addition, we offered a series of laboratory-based programs through the division, largely in association with other consortia of colleges and universities, which produced large numbers of undergraduate and graduate students in the sciences. Other programs brought university scientists to the laboratory for hands-on research with equipment not available within their own institution. Programs such as these were attractive to me in considering the position. The budget to be administered, at least $3 million, was substantially larger than the one for which I was responsible at MSU (approximately $1 million). Frankly, I must also admit to total fascination with the scope of research being done at Argonne. I had never visited the laboratory, yet I was from Chicago. This says nothing about me but a great deal about the nonexistent outreach activities of the laboratory in the 1940s and 1950s. (I did visit the Enrico Fermi Institute at the University of Chicago while studying physics in high school, thanks to my teacher. Of course, Enrico Fermi was the father of nuclear reactors, and Argonne was intimately involved.)

The research underway at Argonne boggled the imagination of a scientist who had not been exposed to anything except university-level research in his own laboratory. At Argonne we saw projects that brought teams of scientists and engineers together to work cooperatively. There was a fairly large magneto-hydrodynamics project underway at the laboratory while I was there. There was the development of an intense pulse neutron source (IPNS) during and after my period at the laboratory. There was the low-level radiation effects study built around women who had worked at the Elgin Watch Company in Elgin, Illinois, many of whom had died prematurely.

The people at Argonne were friendly, and I was particularly impressed with those who would become my immediate staff if I accepted the position. I did accept, and I joined the laboratory in July 1979. I did this despite leaving home at a time when my son was approaching his teen years. Bramlett was twelve, Priscilla eight. These were important years for the children, and going to the laboratory was not an easy decision for me to make. But it was quite an opportunity, and I left with the thought that if things went well we might all go back to my hometown. In short, I was considering a permanent separation from Michigan State, even though I had taken a year's leave of absence.

Ruth and I discussed this transition, and she provided the additional support that helped me make the choice. No doubt I also was motivated by my experience in support programs, where I felt that I had done good work. Argonne offered an opportunity for a reimmersion of sorts in the scientific establishment. I welcomed it! I went forward to it expectantly!

The laboratory met my expectations. Mike Nevitt, deputy director for research, was a very supportive supervisor. I did not anticipate that the leadership of the laboratory was also changing. Walter E. Massey became director of Argonne the same day that I joined. Massey was an African American who had been dean of undergraduate instruction at Brown University. (He would go on to become the vice president for research at the University of Chicago, director of the National Science Foundation, and a vice president at the University of California.) Clearly, in naming an African American to head the laboratory, the Department of Energy and the National Laboratories were moving off in a new direction. I also nourished the thought that Mike Nevitt wanted to impress the new director, in part, and had vigorously sought out an African American to head at least one of the divisions.

One of the larger projects for which we had responsibility was the nuclear power training courses under the auspices of the International Atomic Energy Agency. I will reiterate that the purpose was to assist developing countries in making good decisions about whether nuclear power was an appropriate energy source for them to consider for electric power generation. Roughly four courses a year were taught at Argonne, plus courses at Saclay, near Paris, and at Karlsruhe, Germany; one course was taught in Spain. For each course, 20 or 25 participants from developing countries visited the laboratory. I would welcome the groups, but at the time I knew little about nuclear power, and I did not teach the courses or any part of them. Instead, we contracted with scientists and engineers from the region and around the country to come in to design and teach these courses. There was one incident that jarred what was otherwise a fairly routine set of course offerings under this IAEA project.

One morning, I checked my incoming mail and saw the list of new course participants I would be welcoming later that week. Two were listed as from the "Republic of Africa." I became quite suspicious, since there is no such country. I soon learned that they were coming from the Republic of South Africa, which is a developed country. Needless to say, I was shocked. Developed countries were forbidden to participate in our training courses. When I discussed the matter with the director of the project, I learned that there had been two vacancies in the class that he had been unable to fill. South Africa was interested in having some of its representatives attend, and apparently it was quite within the realm of normal procedure to allow South Africa to be added, even though it was not wise under the circumstances. I still questioned it, and I felt that the matter should be brought immediately to Director Massey's attention. Walter was quite surprised as well. A series of events then rapidly began to occur.

African American staff at the laboratory apparently had gotten wind of the fact that two South Africans were coming and organized a protest. They also wrote a letter of protest to the United Nations, with which the IAEA has a relationship. Walter was quite concerned and wanted the South Africans to leave the laboratory. I met with the delegates and found them to be two very different individuals. One, of English background, was fairly relaxed about the entire affair; the other, an Afrikaner, was quite uptight and wanted to return home to avoid any public attention being brought to himself. I told them they were invited to the Staff Club that evening for a meeting with the director of the laboratory. Walter advised them of the situation that was rapidly developing around their presence at the laboratory. By now, the African American staff protest was in full gear. Coincidentally, I left for my weekend trip to Okemos. While I was away, the South Africans left the laboratory.

That Sunday I received a call from the U. S. Department of State, inquiring into the incident. I was amazed that the news had made its way to Washington so quickly. But that was not all. At this time my wife was on the Study Commission for U. S. Policy Toward Southern Africa, which was meeting with various representatives of different governments, including South Africa. I learned from her that she had been at meetings in which considerable concern had been raised by the South Africans about failure of the U.S. government to support South Africa when efforts were made to unseat it at an international meeting of the IAEA in India. Those efforts were directly related to the incident that had occurred at Argonne, and they obviously were related as well to suspicions that South Africa was not abiding by the rules of the IAEA in the development of nuclear weapons.

At about this time Mike Nevitt and I began to discuss a possible new program that would make it easy for faculty from universities to come to Argonne and spend periods up to a full year engaged in research. How this was created is a lesson in ways to avoid a complex bureaucracy and get a plan implemented in a timely manner. It should be a lesson to university administrators. The program was called the Argonne Faculty Sabbatical Research Leave Program. We wanted to include adequate travel allowances and other salary incentives for participating in this program, so we built them in. Finally, we wanted to ensure that the faculty did not lose access to any of the benefits that accrue to them as regular members of the faculty, such as retirement or health benefits. Therefore, we wanted the faculty to stay fully on the payroll of the university, with Argonne National Laboratory reimbursing the institution for the faculty salary.

We accomplished all this, and we did so in one meeting in my conference room that brought together all the key representatives in personnel, the office of the director, the office of the deputy director, and so forth. Everyone had been provided with basic background information on what we wanted to accomplish. When we met, the goal was to leave that meeting with all the details of the program worked out, including who would sign the contracts with the universities. That was an interesting one. The representatives of the director, when we came to that point, asked what would facilitate the program. The answer was simple. The program would be facilitated and less bureaucratic if the director of the Division of Educational Programs was able to sign all contracts with the universities associated with the program. His response was: "Then we'll see to it that authority is delegated to you." Thus, the Argonne National Laboratory Faculty Sabbatical Research Leave Program was created and successfully implemented in 1979, and I expect it continues to the present day.

Through the IAEA project I was given a substantial exposure to international programs. We brought many students from around the world, including Egypt, India, sub-Saharan Africa, some of the less developed countries of Europe, and Latin America. By and large, the people who came to these courses were involved in electric power generation in their countries at the policy level. We had our own classrooms and other facilities for use by the students. For each class we held a large reception and dinner, and we invited other representatives from across the laboratory. We usually had excellent turnouts for these receptions. I had an opportunity in 1980 to travel to the International Atomic Energy Agency in Vienna, and on the way I visited the training facilities and laboratories at Saclay, France, and at Karlsruhe, West Germany. The trip was my first to Europe, and I was accompanied, once I got to Germany, by the director of Argonne's IAEA project, Manuel Kanter.

I went in May 1980, and after a short stay in Paris as a tourist was taken to Saclay. The staff there was not inclined to give me any view of the Phoenix Breeder Reactor Program. In fact, all that I was able to see at Saclay was the training facility and the educational program. In Frankfurt, Germany, I was met by Manuel Kanter, with whom I drove to meet with the staff at the Karlsruhe Research Laboratory. It was quite reminiscent of Argonne, with the exception that it was surrounded by concertina wire, an indication of the heavy security at this facility. The Germans were quite pleasant and receptive to our visit. One evening we drove into the Black Forest for dinner at a lovely restaurant, where we had venison and delicious accompaniments. The following day I had an extensive tour of the laboratory, as the Germans were much more open in this regard than were the French. In particular, I had the chance to observe a new uranium enrichment process that was being developed for use in Brazil.

From Karlsruhe we went on to Vienna and the meetings with the IAEA committee concerned with the nuclear power training courses. I again saw Dr. Bauer from Paris and those I had met at Karlsruhe, as well as representatives from Spain who were also engaged in the training program. The meeting was chaired by an Italian who was fluent in German, Italian, French, English, and possibly other languages. While I cannot recall his name, he helped to make my stay in Vienna a most delightful one. I also learned that the director of Argonne's IAEA program was tolerated but not very well liked within the IAEA, apparently because of his tendency to dominate the committee meetings.

Back at Argonne, I had hired Dr. Frank M. Vivio from the East West Center in Honolulu as assistant director for my division. I had worked with him at Michigan State. There was some reluctance within the laboratory leadership to hiring a nonscientist, however. Frank's Ph.D. was in education, with a background in evaluation assessment and measurement. In other words, he possessed the relevant quantitative skills. With Frank Vivio on hand I would be freer to engage in additional activities inside and outside the laboratory. One of these was another opportunity to make site visits for the National Science Foundation. This time I was asked to lead the team. The site was Atlanta University, which had received $1.5 million for an NSF Regional Resource Center in Science and Engineering for Minority Students. I was asked to head the group that would assess progress. The director of the center was an old friend, Dr. Thomas Cole, who was also provost at Atlanta University Center. I also met with the president, Dr. Cleveland Dennard. The center was part of a larger consortium of universities in the southeast region, and the project was linked with the City of Atlanta school system through a series of Saturday science academies offered through the resource center. We were impressed. I began to think about ways of linking Argonne to developments in the southeast region.

Argonne's Division of Educational Programs had very few minorities involved in its activities, particularly African Americans, Hispanics, and Native Americans. But there was great interest in including more people from these groups in laboratory activities. In fact, it was during this period that the president of the United States charged every department of government to take an active role in increasing the numbers of underrepresented minorities in their projects and activities. As a result, Argonne accelerated its efforts in this regard. Specifically, I discussed with the staff the development of a relationship with Atlanta University Center's program. We invited about 40 scientists from HBCUs in the Atlanta consortium to visit Argonne and gave them a substantial tour of the facilities and the broadly based multidisciplinary research underway. The laboratory and Atlanta University Center signed a cooperative agreement a year later that would result in more scientists and graduate students from that region coming to Argonne.

The laboratory also became involved in precollege programs with inner-city youth from the greater Chicago area. These students were brought to the laboratory during the summer and housed at North Central College in Naperville, Illinois. As a result, Argonne substantially expanded its interface with the African American and Hispanic communities in the Chicago area.

My tenure at the laboratory was coming to an end. As I reflected upon my experience, it had been everything I had wanted it to be, but it had also been very draining emotionally and physically. When I came to Argonne I lived in Chicago with my uncle, James Jones, and his wife, Sarah, and commuted daily to the laboratory, approximately 40 miles one way. In addition, I made it a point to be home in Okemos as many weekends as possible. I had originally planned to fly home, but the oil crisis and deregulation tripled the fare within two months of my arriving at the laboratory. I managed a few flights to Lansing, but mostly I drove on those weekend trips. I also missed my family, and I was determined that we would be reunited that next year.

My transition back to Michigan State University was facilitated by a telephone call and a letter from Provost Lee Winder, who offered me a position as assistant provost for undergraduate education with responsibility for admissions and scholarships, Military Science, Aerospace Studies, the Undergraduate University Division, the Office of Supportive Services, Office of Programs for Handicapped Students, and Upward Bound. I would become chair of the Undergraduate Assistant/Associate Deans Group. I decided to accept this offer and return to MSU. I had determined that under no conditions would I move my family to Chicago and have my children attend the public schools. The year I was at Argonne was traumatic for me and for the city of Chicago. Virtually every group of city workers either went on strike or threatened to do so—teachers, CTA workers, firemen, and police. It was the reign of Mayor Byrne. The quality of life in Okemos was impressed upon me. Furthermore, I do not think I could have handled another year of separation, with all the emotional and physical drain, so I went back to Michigan State in a new capacity.

▼

CHAPTER SEVEN

BUDGET CRISIS, DECLINING ENROLLMENTS, & ADMINISTERING AT MICHIGAN STATE UNIVERSITY 1980-1985

W hen I returned to MSU in 1980, University College had been dissolved. This had been the home for more than 40 years of the general education program, taught by the Departments of Natural Science, American Thought and Language, Humanities, and Social Science. These faculties had responsibility for 45 credits of general education for all undergraduates. With the dissolution, each department was returned to its home college— Natural Science, Arts and Letters, or Social Science. The faculty continued to teach the same courses in general education until a decade later, when proposals would be made to build a new core curriculum. What remained of University College was an advising and academic progress monitoring unit, renamed the Undergraduate University Division and assigned to me. Willard Warrington was the director. President Cecil Mackey had hired a new vice president—an African American—for student affairs and services. Lee Winder was still provost, and under this new president he expected to have far less time to deal with issues in the office and would have to delegate much more to us. He anticipated that President Mackey would make sweeping changes and that his administrative style would be to delegate much more to his executive officers.

In the Office of the Provost we moved ahead to perform our duties as effectively and efficiently as possible in anticipation of the new order. Many of the recommendations contained in the Supportive Services Advisory Report were being implemented. For instance, the organization's name was changed to the College Achievement Admission Program, and Delores Reed, who was my administrative secretary, became the administrative assistant for budgetary matters. I hired a new secretary, Barbara VanBalen. I also managed to negotiate new space for me and my immediate staff. Delores, Barbara, and I occupied offices outside the Administration Building for the first time. We moved to the second floor of Bessey Hall, to offices formerly occupied by the dean of University College, Richard Carlin. This was an ideal and quite comfortable suite, although we missed the informal encounters in the Administration Building through which so much business could be conducted.

I also had administrative responsibility for all undergraduate admissions to Michigan State University. Charles Seeley, the director of Admissions and Scholarships, reported to me.

This was a difficult time for the university. The Board of Trustees had declared a fiscal crisis; we were anticipating major budget reductions and even the elimination of programs and academic units. Cecil Mackey had, in fact, been brought to MSU in part to deal with these fiscal issues. He appointed a select committee to examine the situation; it recommended program deletions and elimination of the colleges of Urban Development, James Madison, and Lyman Briggs. Justin Morrill College had already been dismantled in part. The committee also suggested closing the College of Nursing. Other candidates for cuts or elimination included the Honors Program, Landscape Architecture, and Urban Planning. The recommendations were discussed within the academic governance system and, as the Coordinated Proposal, were presented to the Board of Trustees. Once that occurred the recommendations were in the public domain. There was considerable dismay in all the units proposed for elimination, and they organized to present their respective cases.

Public meetings of the Board of Trustees were scheduled in such places as the Brody Complex Multipurpose Room, which could accommodate hundreds of people. Indeed, hundreds turned out for some of these sessions, attended by large numbers of external constituents of the threatened programs. In that atmosphere, the

Board of Trustees backed away from the eliminations being proposed by the administration and instead developed the Modified Coordinated Proposal, which was significantly less drastic.

We did lose the College of Urban Development in this process. The college and its dean, Dr. Robert L. Green, had emerged from the old Center for Urban Affairs in the mid-1970s. It included two departments—Urban and Metropolitan Studies, and Racial and Ethnic Studies. In addition, the unit had retained an urban affairs outreach component. Green was on leave when this program elimination was proposed and had to fight it from Chicago. He was unsuccessful. Urban Development, which had never reached the enrollment level of 800-1,000 that might have helped sustain it, was lost to MSU and the African American student population it had served. This elimination left a number of unmet needs in undergraduate education for minority and majority students at Michigan State. In its place, Urban Affairs Programs was established at the graduate level, with its own dean, plus the Equal Opportunity Fellowship Program, the Affirmative Action Graduate Assistants Program, and other minority fellowship programs that had been in the Graduate School. That school, which under Dean Oyer's leadership had been developing into a highly centralized and stronger unit, was cut back significantly. Dean Oyer soon left MSU for his original institution, Ohio State. The EOP programs that were moved were the same that I had administered while assistant dean of the Graduate School.

The search to find units to eliminate or reduce continued to be a priority at Michigan State for some time. I was visited in 1980 by the deans of the colleges of Arts and Letters, Social Science, and Natural Science; all came right to the point. They wanted Undergraduate University Division dissolved. They saw this unit as serving no purpose not could not be served just as well by reallocating resources to the various colleges. I was not surprised. This was part of what had become a continuous assault against the old University College, which many thought had outlived its usefulness. The Undergraduate University Division, which now reported to me, was all that was left. As noted earlier, the instructional departments had been transferred to their respective colleges.

I resisted the deans' suggestions and told them that the needs of our undergraduates, particularly those who entered MSU undecided about their major (no-preference students), were best served by a centralized academic affairs office. I also noted that if we had one College of Arts and Sciences I would be less concerned. I also pointed out that even those students who had declared a major but were in the lower division received academic advising to a very large degree from the Undergraduate University Division. There was no further pressure from the deans to disband the division, and it survived the budget reduction discussions.

In the midst of this, the provost let me know that he wanted my immediate staff to return to the fourth floor of the Administration Building. After some consideration I concurred, but only under the condition that I get more space than the small office that I had occupied for my first 10 years. This was agreed, and I moved to room 443 of the Administration Building. Delores Reed occupied 442, and my secretary was in 444. It was good to be back under these improved conditions, which I had grown accustomed to at Argonne National Laboratory.

The Modified Coordinated Proposal finally was acted upon, and our programs felt the axe, along with others across the university. Some faculty positions were lost, but thanks to Mordechai Kreinin, a professor of economics, most of these occurred through faculty buy-outs and early retirements under a program he suggested to the Academic Council. MSU received a considerable amount of negative publicity as a result of its very public efforts to eliminate programs. As the individual with administrative responsibility for admissions, I was quite concerned. For fall 1981 we experienced a 6.2 percent reduction in undergraduate enrollment. These losses were a consequence of poor retention—students who had been enrolled not returning to the university—and of a drop in first-time freshman enrollment. Some people in Admissions were convinced that a major reason for the decline was all the negative publicity about possible program eliminations. Prospective students were uncertain what would be available at MSU. We were not allowed to assert this publicly, so we talked about other contributing factors, but I am convinced to this day that this was the biggest single factor.

In the final analysis, the only college to be eliminated was the College of Urban Development, which had served African American students and some foreign and majority students. The college had offered a series of courses in racial and ethnic studies, and these were lost to the curriculum and, indeed, have never been replaced. This was, no doubt, a political decision motivated by long-standing opposition in the legislature to the creation and funding for the college and its predecessor, the Center for Urban Affairs. Dean Robert L. Green returned to campus in fall 1981 and rejoined the Council of Deans. These meetings were most disturbing, as it was clear that there was considerable antagonism between Dean Green and President Mackey and that Bob Green was having great difficulty adjusting to this changed situation, which significantly altered the opportunities available to African American students and others enrolled at MSU.

Personally, I had never thought that a College of Urban Development was a good idea, but the racial and ethnic studies curriculum did serve a useful purpose. In the 1970s my wife, Ruth, a faculty member in the Department of Sociology, had proposed a college built around Black Diasporan Studies, but this idea was rejected by staff in the provost's office. Bob Green abandoned the concept under pressure from Dorothy Arata, John Dietrich, and the provost. That was a major turning point for African American students and faculty at MSU. Years later, under a different provost—David Scott—MSU would establish and fund the Julian Samora Institute, which would be quite successful in meeting the needs for Hispanic American research within the university, and subsequently Ruth developed the African Diaspora Research Project. This graduate-level research program obtained funding from the Ford Foundation and modest support from MSU; it was and is housed in Urban Affairs Programs and continues to enjoy local, national, and international attention. Urban Affairs Programs, under the leadership of Dean Joe Darden, and the College of Social Science have, over the years, provided support for the African Diaspora Research Project, but broader needs of African American faculty, undergraduates, and graduate students interested in African American studies at MSU have not fared as well. This has been a dilemma at the undergraduate level, because the Urban Affairs Programs have been oriented essentially to service the needs of graduate studies and their service components.

▼   ▼   ▼

In fall 1981, following a decline of 6.2 percent in undergraduate enrollment, the associate provost established two task forces, one on admissions and recruitment and the other on retention. As assistant provost for undergraduate education, I chaired the Task Force on Recruitment. We brought together a range of people from across central administration, including Steve Terry, assistant vice president; Chuck Seeley, director of Admissions and Scholarships; Tom Scarlett, director of the Office of Financial Aids; Florence Harris, director of the Office of Supportive Services; and a number of others. We met many times over a period of several weeks, trying to understand the factors that had contributed to the decline in first-time freshmen and in returning students. There was little doubt in our minds that a major reason was the negative publicity, mentioned earlier. But, nonetheless, we plowed through a great amount of information seeking to come to an understanding of this issue.

Our Task Force developed a 12-point plan for dealing with the problems confronting recruitment at MSU.

1. An all-university Open House in the spring to which thousands of high school students and their parents would be invited
2. High school and community college visits
3. Alumni recruitment program
4. Cooperative Extension program
5. Telephone contacts with admitted students
6. Letters from academic units
7. Financial aid award letters to new students
8. Admission of students for whom decisions have been withheld (WDs)
9. Use of Visa or MasterCard for advance enrollment deposits

10. Use of the toll-free line within admissions
11. Radio announcements
12. Television coverage

The plan was reasonably well received within central adminis-tration, and the office of Admissions and Scholarships moved ahead to implement it. One of my own contributions was to estab-lish a minority admissions and recruitment unit within the Admissions and Scholarships office that would bring together all of those involved in minority admissions for improved coordination and analysis.

It was becoming clear that the director of Admissions and Scholarships did not wish to work within the new administrative configuration. He resigned and went to the Carolinas, where he became admissions director at another institution. A search was instituted by me to find a replacement. I was assisted by Dr. Barbara Steidle, who wrote to several institutions inquiring about highly qualified directors or associate directors of admissions whom we should seek for this position. The choice was Dr. William Turner, director of Admissions and Scholarships, Washington University in St. Louis. Bill joined us in 1983 and hit the ground running.

We were in the throes of implementing the recommendations of the task force for improving the recruitment of undergraduate stu-dents to Michigan State. I advertised our first Open House in April 1982, publicized by radio announcements across the state. This was an upbeat event, meant to raise people out of the doldrums of the budget reduction. That first Open House was in Munn Ice Arena; every college in the university, as well as all the major academic support units, put on exhibits for our guests. We ran bus tours of the campus, and at several points the visitors could get off the buses and visit facilities or classes. The press turned out in great numbers. It was historic, but not quite so historic as I had thought. When I referred to Madison Kuhn's history of Michigan State, I learned that at the turn of the century there were annual excursions to the university by prospective students, who were met by cadets with horses and wagons and taken on tours of the campus. Our Open

House was not new after all, but the rebirth in modern times of an older idea!

The Open House was quite successful. We had arranged for some units that regularly held their own Open Houses—such as the College of Veterinary Medicine and the College of Engineering—to schedule their open houses during the same week, which increased the number of visitors to the campus. President Mackey took a ride on the buses to get a flavor of the event. TV coverage was full of positive messages from our visitors about the Open House. There was little question in my mind that it went a long way in allaying prospective enrollees' concerns that MSU was in the process of eliminating some of its more attractive and desirable programs. The event became a regular feature of the university's recruitment program for the next decade. While it would be reduced from the original four or five days to two or three, the numbers of visitors would remain high. Open House Programs were continued under the leadership of Bill Turner, who joined the university on February 1, 1983.

The recruitment task force's 12-point plan met its overall goal the very next year, when the decline in freshman enrollment stopped. The task force studying retention of enrolled undergraduates issued a more complex report. There were, in fact, no major problems in retention of the general undergraduate population. There were difficulties in certain areas, particularly among minority students, so the recommendations tended to focus on these as well as areas that potentially could affect the larger undergraduate population. I prepared interim reports on the results of implementation of the recommendations of this task force, which was chaired by Associate Provost Jack B. Kinsinger.

Another upbeat activity that raised the spirits of faculty, staff, and students was the opening of the Clifton and Dolores Wharton Center for the Performing Arts. The Chicago Symphony came to perform. A real highlight was the warm welcome given to the Whartons when they stood before the audience in the Great Hall.

▼   ▼   ▼

Some final comments are in order regarding President Cecil Mackey, who came to MSU in 1979. He had previously served as president at Texas Tech University in Lubbock. He would lead MSU for five years, under conditions that stood out in sharp contrast to those faced by previous presidents. The university was experiencing severe financial problems, and he had been selected, in part, because of his demonstrated ability to lead a university through a period of financial stress. This he sought to do, and vigorously. He brought with him Ken Thompson as vice president for operations, and Ken assumed major responsibility for setting a new direction for MSU in dealing with its financial circumstances. Lee Winder continued as provost and played a larger role in dealing with financial and academic matters during the tenure of President Mackey.

President Mackey deserves credit for addressing MSU's fiscal problems through a series of program eliminations, but, as noted earlier, most of those never occurred. Instead, a Modified Coordinated Proposal was developed which provided for such things as early retirements and buy-outs of some faculty, administrators, and staff (the ideas put forward as an alternative approach by Mordechai Kreinin, Distinguished Professor of Economics at MSU). Yet, President Mackey was effective in hiring minorities and was recognized for this by a local black fraternity, Alpha Chi Boule, at a large reception in his honor at the Lansing Country Club. President Mackey appointed Moses Turner as the first African American vice president (Student Affairs and Services) in the history of MSU. During the Mackey years, three Blacks were appointed as department chairs: Donald Williams in Psychiatry, Barbara Ross-Lee in Family Medicine, and Ernest Moore in Audiology and Speech Sciences.

President Mackey also was responsible for reorganizing university relations with its alumni. The reorganization gave individual colleges and departments more control over alumni affairs. These changes in the alumni organization were reacted to negatively by the head of the association and by many alumni across the country, as well as the national association.

The major accomplishment of President Mackey's administration was to set MSU on a realistic path for dealing with its financial situation. (We had all failed to see the handwriting on the wall in the 1972 oil crisis and the long-term effect of competition from Japanese automobile producers on the economy of Michigan.) A major failure was the inability to realize the political implications of severe cutbacks and not to plan accordingly. The whole approach, in my opinion, was also forged in part by a desire to move MSU toward becoming an AAU research university of the first order, rather than to continue to build on the strengths of the institution in the area of undergraduate education and public service.

▼   ▼   ▼

Despite the fiscal crisis, the budget reductions, and my leave of absence, 1980-85 were relatively good years for the support programs that I had begun at MSU—the Office of Supportive Services and the Office of Programs for Handicapper Students. Judy Taylor Gentile continued as director of the OPHS, as did Florence Harris for OSS. Each program was fortunate that federal funds continued to flow and provide essential support. By this time there had been an increase in access to the OSS for those who were the first generation in their family to attend college. The handicapper program benefited from a new federal law in the late 1970s that mandated accessibility for handicapper students on university and college campuses across the country. Although Michigan State was not in compliance (Edgar Harden, who had succeeded Clifton Wharton, had to grapple with this new legislation), it was in much better shape than most schools. This was due in no small measure to Judy Gentile. (She and Eric Gentile had been married in the Horticulture Gardens adjacent to the Student Services Building. The ceremony was absolutely beautiful, and I was pleased to have been asked to participate.) Both Judy and Eric had significantly pressed an agenda for access for handicappers and beyond, for that matter. These two outstanding individuals attracted super people to work for and with them.

Florence Harris began to develop such a substantial staff with the resources made available to her that the Holden Hall suite became too restricted. We were able to get new space in Erickson Hall and establish a formal tutorial center as well as a computer laboratory, filled with Macintosh microcomputers, for use by students served by OSS.

The movement of Judy Gentile from quarters in the Library to what was at the time probably the most accessible structure on campus—the Communication Arts and Sciences Building—was an achievement for which she and Eric alone deserve credit. To this day, I do not know how they brought it off, other than by the sheer force of their personalities. This new facility was equipped with excellent elevators of the right size, the appropriate signage for handicappers, and graded entry to the main building. I can recall them embarking upon Project Access, made possible in the mid-1970s by funding from the Board of Trustees. To our good fortune, the State of Michigan matched these funds. Under Project Access we mounted on a broad scale the installation of campus pathway ramps and accessible lavatory facilities in classroom buildings and dormitories. We were not able to tackle the Union Building for a long time, because of its multiple levels of entry, but the impossible finally was achieved when a quite elegant extended ramp was installed in the 1980s, along with an accessible elevator to move from the lower cafeteria level to the study lounge level.

By now Judy Gentile had expanded the services of OPHS to include two very different but significant populations: those with learning characteristics and those with hearing characteristics. With the marriage of Judy and Eric, it was also necessary to separate the two of them so that a spouse was not supervising a spouse. This was achieved with the transfer of Eric to the Department of Human Relations to head up a new program for handicappers and veterans.

By the 1980s Florence Harris had taken the leadership in the preparation of the OSS proposal that went to Washington. The model had been set years earlier, and while the size of the proposal had expanded, we now received funding for three years instead of one. When Florence and Judy began preparing proposals, we had entered the computer age, whereas Delores Reed and I had prepared ours on typewriters. We typically had to send as many as five copies to Washington, and Delores would prepare stencils that we would run on mimeograph machines. Usually we worked on proposals to the final day, and I would then fly them to Washington. As I reflect upon the many hours we put in working on these proposals, which literally brought millions of dollars to the university, I am amazed that we had the stamina.

Florence Harris in OSS and Glenda Hammond in Upward Bound were also playing a much larger role in managing their programs as well as in the affairs of the MAEOPP. Glenda had been appointed director after Keith Williams became director of academic orientation programs in the Office of Admissions and Scholarships. By now, we also had a national organization made up of regional associations from across the nation, including Alaska, Hawaii, and Puerto Rico: the National Council of Educational Opportunity Associations (NCEOA). Arnold Mitchem, the major architect, moved up to become its executive director. Florence Harris was readily received by the traditional leadership and other wise men and women of the association. She showed a fundamental intelligence and quickness of thought that I deemed essential in someone involved as a manager of our program. My faith in her has been redeemed year after year. She is independent, but I have never had a problem with independence so long as it is combined with a healthy share of good common sense.

I continued to serve both MAEOPP and NCEOA. For the latter I functioned as a major trainer in federally funded workshops sponsored over several years in various parts of the country. For one of these I prepared workbooks on model programs in science for Upward Bound and Special Services Programs.

▼

CHAPTER EIGHT

INTERNATIONAL PROGRAMS AT THE NATIONAL SCIENCE FOUNDATION

While I had done a fair amount of work for the National Science Foundation over the years, Walter Massey, director of Argonne National Laboratory, provided me with the unusual opportunity of serving on the Committee on International Programs within the NSF. Part of a directorate within the foundation, the Office of International Programs, had a modest budget but managed a number of international relationships between the U.S. government and/or NSF and other governments and/or peer agencies around the world, and there were some multilateral relationships as well. The director of the office was Dr. Boda Bartocha. I was quite pleased to be appointed to this committee based on Walter's recommendation (he also served at this time on the National Science Board, which had oversight of NSF).

I looked forward to attending my first meeting, where I was surprised to find that the body included all white males. The chair was a professor from the University of Texas at Austin, and the other members were drawn from major research universities and the private sector in the Washington, D.C., area. Initially I knew very little about the committee's work. My exposure to international programs had been slight at Michigan State but somewhat greater at Argonne National Laboratory, through my work with the International Atomic Energy Agency.

The NSF director at this time was an African American, Dr. James G. Slaughter, an engineer from Washington State University.

121

He joined us in the afternoon and made a presentation reflecting his desire to see a sub-Saharan Africa program established. It was an excellent opportunity to meet such a distinguished individual, who handled himself extremely well. He is what I would call "cool, calm, and collected."

It was when he left that a problem arose. The member from Georgetown University made a reference, during a discussion of South Africa, to the "Hottentots." I did not think I had heard right, but he repeated it, and everyone was amused by his comment except me. I felt the need to tell him that the term never should be used when referring to the African people of South Africa, for it is considered to be a racial slur (the correct name for these people is Khoi-Khoin). My statement led to a very quiet meeting for the rest of the afternoon, but never was there another effort to make sport of either Africans or African Americans during my tenure on that committee.

NSF hired Bob Bell to direct the sub-Saharan Africa program. Bob traveled extensively in the region and reported to our committee over time. In 1983 Dr. Slaughter requested that I visit Kenya and Nigeria on behalf of NSF, and I arranged a stop in Geneva, Switzerland, to break the long trip. From there I flew to Nairobi for an international meeting sponsored by the Regional Office of Science and Technology for Africa (ROSTA) as well as a conference sponsored by UNESCO/ROSTA, "Public Understanding of Science and a Regional Plan for Scientific and Technological Exchanges in African Countries." I was to present a paper entitled "International Cooperation in Science and Technology—Problems and Perspectives" at this conference. I also was to arrange through the U.S. Embassy for a meeting with Minister Ngeno, head of Kenya's Ministry of Science and Technology.

Nairobi was a beautiful city. I had been scheduled into the Hilton Hotel, but the driver who picked me up had other plans. He took me to a much older hotel owned by an Indian family, and while it was comfortable, it was not what I had expected. I checked in and walked toward downtown, where I saw that the Hilton was blocked off by security guards. A meeting of the Organization of African Unity had brought heads of state to the city. I showed my passport and after being searched went into the Hilton and checked on whether they had a reservation for me. They did, and I advised them of what had happened. They called the other hotel and arranged for my bags to be brought over. Of course, I returned and packed my bags and came back with them. The Hilton was quite comfortable, and I was able to handle the food there with no problems. During the remainder of the day I walked around the city and saw the tomb of the former president of Kenya, Jomo Kenyatta, and the center where I thought our conference would meet. The center consisted of a very tall building adjacent to a traditional hut, which was the main conference facility. It turned out that the offices of Minister Ngeno were in the taller building.

I did not attempt to visit Ngeno at this time but instead proceeded to the U.S. Embassy, as I had been advised to do by the NSF. I was shocked to find that the Marine guards would not allow me to enter the building. I stood on the other side of a large, bullet-proof window and passed across my passport and letters of introduction from the NSF. As an ex-Marine traveling for NSF, this was hard to take. I became quite angry the longer I cooled my heels outside the embassy, and I did not get in that day.

The following day I made my way up to Bruce House and the UNESCO/ROSTA conference, which began more or less on schedule. I met a number of African scientists, one of whom was from Nairobi, a professor of electrical engineering at the university. I shared my experience at the embassy with him and noted that I needed an appointment with Minister Ngeno. We climbed into the professor's car, drove to the U.S. Embassy, proceeded through the back service entrance, and were let in with no problems. Within a few minutes I was walking around inside, unescorted, while before with good credentials I had been unable to get in the main gate. What an irony! I was eventually able to gain access through the front door, but only after more complaints. The individual with whom I met was an economics officer—a junior-level position—not the ambassador. He said he would try to arrange a meeting for me with the minister, but he did not think this would be possible. The economics officer was kind enough to invite me to his home for dinner.

I returned to the conference to listen to the other papers and present my own. The papers were all quite interesting, and I believe that mine was reasonably well received. It was at this time that my friend, the electrical engineer, took me to the offices of Minister Ngeno. We went past all the security points manned by armed guards, all of whom were known to my new friend, and he made a point of introducing me. When we got up to the office, the minister was not in, but my friend knew the secretary quite well, and she scheduled an appointment for me on the following Monday. I did not inform the Embassy of this, but later they somehow learned about it, and they were most curious about how it had been arranged. I was reluctant to share this information with them. They asked that I meet with them again, after my meeting with the minister.

On Saturday I went off on my only pleasure trip during the visit to Kenya, to Amboseli Game Reserve near the Tanzania border, at the foot of Mt. Kilimanjaro. This was a delightful trip, and I recommend it highly. Kilimanjaro is an impressive mountain, and a large number of animals live at its base on the fauna and the water that flows from the snowy peak.

When I returned to the city on Sunday afternoon, I had not been in my room an hour before it was time to join my friend in the Embassy for dinner. He met me at the hotel and took me out to his home, which was quite pleasant. He had a lovely family, including a young son and daughter. We had cocktails and chatted, and I finally told him how I came to have the meeting with Minister Ngeno. It was then that I began to understand that U. S. Embassy personnel are not always readily received by host governments and are not necessarily in a good position to arrange meetings with government ministers. We had a good meal, and I returned to my hotel to rest up for my encounter the next day with Minister Ngeno.

My meeting with the minister was successful. He had several other representatives join us, and we discussed some of the bilateral relationships in science that they would like to see established between the United States and Kenya. Of course, I made extensive notes and reported to the NSF upon my return.

To my great surprise I was invited back to the Embassy on the very day I was to leave for the airport. I knew this was to find out what had been discussed with Minister Ngeno. I went to the meeting in an Embassy car with my bags packed, and I met the U.S. ambassador and key members of his staff. He was most gracious. I was still frustrated by my treatment by the Marine guards on that first day, and the ambassador was most apologetic. He was too nice a man to remain angry with for very long. We had a gracious visit and conversation. I shared information with him on my meeting with the Minister of Science and Technology and then had to rush to the airport in the ambassador's vehicle. I believe it is correct to say that my trip to Nairobi was quite eventful, never dull, most interesting, and for the NSF I believe it was informative.

From Nairobi, I flew by Ethiopian Airlines into Lagos, Nigeria. What a large boom town! We arrived at night, and I was met by representatives of the Minister of Science and Technology, which was fortunate. There were check points all around the airport manned by armed military guards, and if you did not have the right papers, there was no telling what might happen to you. We passed through with no problems because we had a government vehicle. I was taken to my hotel in Lagos and settled in for the night.

The next day I visited with members of the Nigerian Universities Association, the chancellor of Lagos University, and the Minister of Science and Technology, Mr. Oloroporuko, and his immediate staff. We discussed a range of things over tea. There was great interest in Nigeria in nuclear power as an energy source. We discussed environmental issues, biomass, and other related topics particular to the African continent, as well as ways in which U.S. science and technology could be helpful. There was also serious concern raised by the minister that Nigeria was being viewed by the United States as an oil-rich nation with excellent foreign exchange. They said this was not the case, and they should continue to be regarded as a developing country. It was a very, very good meeting. But shortly after I returned home in December 1984, I learned early in the new year that Nigeria had another military coup, which meant that Minister Oloroporuko was no longer in service.

▼   ▼   ▼

Another opportunity to visit Africa came in 1985, this time under the auspices of the American Association for the Advancement of Science. I had met Thomas Ratchford, head of their international programs office, who had served for a while on the International Programs Advisory Committee of the NSF. The AAAS for many years had been sponsoring international conferences. The one in Africa was to be held near Abidjan, Ivory Coast, and I was most interested in participating. This was arranged through the cooperation of Thomas Ratchford and Walter Massey at Argonne.

In December I traveled directly to Dakar, Senegal, where I spent two days visiting MSU research facilities nearby. I also ran into Alfred Opubor, formerly director of the African Studies Center at Michigan State, and was quite surprised to see him. Alfred was working with the Pan-Africa News Agency in Dakar, which we visited, and we went about sampling a bit of the night life as well. I met with various researchers at the MSU facility, and we had a lovely reception at the home of one of them. When he and his family returned to Michigan State, his daughter would attend Okemos High School and become friends with my daughter. It is, indeed, a small world!

I flew on to Abidjan, where I took a bus to the conference facility at Grand Bassam. It had been constructed to house oil workers on a development project near the coast, became a white elephant, and was converted to this use. I was assigned a roommate from Burkina Faso, fluent in English and French, and we had some nice conversations about the ongoing conference. There were representatives of science and technology from all across Africa, the United States, and Europe. For example, the president of the American Chemical Society was there, as was the president of the National Association of Microbiologists, as well as delegates from the Max Planck Institute in Germany, among others. This was a high-ranking group of professionals, and I was quite pleased to be among them. The French, despite their good knowledge of English, insisted that everything be translated simultaneously into French, including the discussions in workshops, where there was no centralized translation facility as in the main conference room. This did not disadvantage us too much.

The conference was opened with pomp and circumstance. The Ivory Coast's Minister of Science and Technology, a very gracious person, arrived accompanied by dancers who performed outside the facility. This was quite impressive and added a different character to the conference. Opening remarks were given by Thomas Ratchford, Walter Massey, and representatives of the Association of Science of the Ivory Coast. We then broke out into subgroups, where we presented our papers and began our discussions on the role of professional societies in science and technology policy in sub-Saharan Africa. That was our theme, and we vigorously pursued it.

I took a large number of photographs at the conference, some of which were published in the proceedings volume, and I received a photo credit. The book appeared under the auspices of AAAS/AFCI.

The conference was a great success. There were a number of major recommendations, which I list here with my comments.

1. Scientific and engineering societies in sub-Saharan Africa should be strengthened, and in those areas where they do not exist and where a demonstrated need exists they should be initiated. There was concern for the development of a stronger scientific infrastructure in sub-Saharan Africa. When I had traveled earlier to East Africa and Nigeria, we were seeking to determine the extent of existence of counterparts to the National Academy of Sciences, the National Science Foundation, and so forth.

2. Effective programs of cooperation and exchange are needed between sub-Saharan African scientific and engineering societies and their counterparts in developing and industrialized countries.

3. Communications are critical to an effective scientific and technical infrastructure in sub-Saharan African, and societies can contribute to their improvement. Here there was interest in

strengthening journal publications and, indeed, in the creation of a major journal for sub-Saharan Africa. Two things occurred as a specific result of this recommendation. Professional societies in the United States and Europe agreed to print extra copies of their journals and circulate them through diplomatic pouches to professional societies in sub-Saharan Africa. In addition, since the conference in 1985, *Discovery and Innovation,* a new journal in science and technology for sub-Saharan Africa, has been developed and is now in the second year of publication under the auspices of the African Academy of Sciences.

4. Scientific and engineering societies can play a strong role in education and training of scientists and engineers in sub-Saharan Africa.

5. Popularization of science and technology is an important complimentary activity to the education and training of scientists and engineers. It provides a pool of potential entrants into the fields of science and technology, as well as providing the public with an understanding of science and engineering in the context of traditions and culture.

6. Scientific and engineering societies should work to establish linkages among industry, universities, and government.

These were the major recommendations flowing from the conference, and they received the unanimous support of all participants. After farewells we boarded planes, and I flew off to Madrid, where I spent two days and nights to break the trip home.

▼

CHAPTER NINE

PRESIDENT DIBIAGGIO MEETS MICHIGAN STATE UNIVERSITY 1986-1989

In 1986 Dr. John DiBiaggio, former president of the University of Connecticut, became the 17th president of Michigan State University. He was an experienced fundraiser and also had experience dealing with state legislatures. I first met the new president at a reception, where Vice President Connie Stewart introduced us. I wanted to be nominated for the next Harvard University Institute on Educational Management (IEM), and President DiBiaggio's administrative aide, David Kimball, saw to it that the letter was written. I was accepted for the summer 1986 IEM.

During President DiBiaggio's tenure, Provost Lee Winder was succeeded by Dr. David Scott, the deputy director of the MSU cyclotron and Hannah Distinguished Professor of Chemistry, Physics, and the Superconducting Cyclotron Laboratory. David had been associate provost. A new era was ushered in by Scott, who listened and learned quickly. Under his tenure we continued to receive excellent support for supportive services and handicapper student programs. It was clear, even in 1983 when Winder appointed Scott as associate provost, that he had picked his own successor.

David Scott selected as his associate provost Lou Anna Kimsey Simon, who was at the time, serving as assistant provost for academic services. I had been a candidate for the associate provost position, and I attribute my lack of success to the fact that I did not have sufficient relevant experience and also did not take the matter seriously enough. I could have had much stronger references and could have pressed for and gotten support from various quarters of the faculty. In addition, I should have prepared more thoroughly for the meetings and interviews with the deans and the selection committee.

▼   ▼   ▼

In 1986 I initiated the university-wide foreign teaching assistant orientation and training program. A series of surveys of undergraduates compiled for me by James McComb showed the need. One had probed undergraduate perceptions of MSU experiences, and in written comments supplementary to the objective survey instrument, many students noted the poor English skills of foreign TAs, particularly in mathematics courses. Within a year there also were similar criticisms from the state legislature. As a direct result, the Office of the Provost funded a foreign TA orientation and training program.

I called upon Dr. Joseph Cousins of the Center for International Studies and Programs to design and set up the first program. Joe had a high degree of enthusiasm, knowledge of international students and their experiences, and ability to proceed with a minimum of direction. He outlined a two-week program. In the first week, staff assessed English competency and oriented the TAs to MSU policies and practices. The second week focused on effective teaching. To assist him, Joe brought together a small staff: Mary Ann Weifrich, Karen Machinchick, Yousri Mahmud Ali, and Amy Purvis. Their very first venture set the pattern for the future program, which would be handled by the individual we hired. Dr. William Rittenberg came to MSU in January 1987 as coordinator of this program, and a faculty advisory committee works closely with the project. It has now been operating for six years, and there is discussion of expanding the orientation and training to all new TAs, foreign and domestic.

From the beginning, the program was closely coordinated with the Graduate School and with academic units. It was designed as a supplement to, not a replacement for, efforts in the various departments, schools, and colleges. It was a welcome and needed addition.

In addition to the language skills issue, many students had complained that foreign TAs lacked awareness of the focus of higher education in the United States. Many were too strict and had extremely high expectations because they came from more competitive systems.

▼   ▼   ▼

In 1986 we launched the High School Scholars Program, modeled after the Principal Scholars Program at the University of Illinois, and designed for middle school or high school youth from underrepresented minority groups. The plan was to identify 50 9th-graders the first year and add 50 more each year until we reached a steady state of 200. Dr. Barbara O'Kelley agreed to manage the program with the understanding that we would have to seek subsequent funding external to the university. Barbara did an excellent job in organizing the first program. Groups of students came for a one-day visit during the academic year, and while we wanted week-long residential programs in the summer, we had no funds for it. The first program was quite successful. We held it in Case Hall, and both parents and students participated. Dr. John Greene of the Department of Religious Studies made a presentation about what is required in high school to be successful at college work. Barbara Steidle, dean of James Madison College, also participated in this first program. Staff from the Office of Admissions and Scholarships also provided assistance. I had great plans for this program and hoped to find external funding for it. We did not know that parallel developments were taking place at the state level that would make this possible.

State Representative Morris Hood had joined with the presidents of Wayne State University, the University of Michigan, and Eastern Michigan University to design a statewide program similar to the MSU High School Scholars Program. The year after our program began, the Martin Luther King, Jr.-Cesar Chavez-Rosa Parks (MLK-CC-RP) College Day Program came into being. The Office of Minority Equity in the Michigan Department of Education administered it. My office received more than $200,000 for this effort to reach youth in grades 7-11 drawn from school districts within 80 miles or more of the university. Thus, MSU served students from Detroit and such urban centers as Flint, Saginaw, and Jackson. This new venture had many characteristics of the federal Talent Search program. MSU mainly served African Americans, Hispanics, and Native Americans, although other underrepresented minorities and white students could be included if they were enrolled in the classes from which we drew our students. Every university in the state received funds to manage one of these programs. One year MSU reached more than 5,000 students. The program now serves about 2,000 annually, and there is both an academic year and a summer component. Elements of the original MSU High School Scholars Program have been retained under a new name, Rising Stars, within the College Day Program, directed as of 1989 by Dr. Pamela Bellamy.

The state initiative also included the MLK-CC-RP Visiting Professor Program, whereby underrepresented minority faculty could spend up to one year teaching at MSU. This program has been carried out at MSU under the leadership of Assistant Provost Robert Banks. The Graduate School administers the MLK-CC-RP Fellowship Program, which continues to provide Ph.D. candidates from minority backgrounds with up to $25,000 in support.

▼   ▼   ▼

In 1986 the university was encouraged to undertake a new program in undergraduate research participation for African American, Hispanic, and Native American students. This encouragement came from the Committee on Institutional Cooperation (CIC), a consortium of the Big Ten and the University of Chicago. The CIC had developed a proposal for a Summer Research Opportunity Program (SROP) to send to the Lilly, Kellogg, and Mellon foundations, seeking support for administrative costs, undergraduate research, and faculty research allowances. Provost Winder placed this new program in my office, and so I organized a session for summer 1986. Initial funding came from the Office of the Provost. The intent was to identify and fund 10 students that summer. Lisa Chavis from the Office of Admissions and Scholarships worked with me in a part-time capacity. I modeled SROP after the undergraduate research programs that I had administered at Argonne National Laboratory in 1979 and 1980. We had students engaged in research in the physical and biological sciences, music, and the social and behavioral sciences. We arranged a series of workshops on "preparing for graduate school" that were run parallel with the research participation activities. At the end of the summer each student reported on his/her research. While most students came with prepared papers and used overhead transparencies or slides, one arrived with trombone and tuba players. His research had involved rewriting some music for those instruments, and his report included a recital.

The first SROP was quite successful. Lisa Chavis helped me the next summer as well, and then I moved SROP under the responsibility of Ms. Florence Harris, director of the Office of Supportive Services. We then learned that more funds for research participation programs would become available from the U.S. Department of Education TRIO programs. We applied and obtained funding for the Ronald E. McNair Post-Baccalaureate Achievement Program, which had the same purposes as SROP. Minority research participation grew over the next several years from the 10 students in the original pilot to more than 55 students in the combined CIC SROP and McNair programs. MSU provided matching funds for SROP, and each student had a $3,000 stipend and each faculty mentor a $500 research allowance. The McNair Program provided up to $2,400 in support—the university added $600 per student to bring them to the same level as the SROP students. (Unlike SROP, this program served low-income students no matter what their racial/ethnic background.) The two programs have proven their worth. We have had students from the very first who have opted to go on and study for the Ph.D. as a direct result of their participation. The programs also have helped bring faculty into collaborative work with underrepresented minority students. Programs like this should be greatly expanded to reach even more students.

▼   ▼   ▼

For a full decade, the Office of Supportive Services had also seen the need and had requested support for a summer College Achievement Admission Program (CAAP). Several institutions in Michigan already had summer components in their programs. During the 1987-88 academic year we sought funding from the Michigan Office of Minority Equity for such an effort and obtained $132,000 to implement the Summer Undergraduate Program Encouraging Retention (SUPER). It was directed at students admitted through CAAP, who were largely African Americans, Chicanos, Hispanics, and Native Americans. From the outset we involved the faculty, since the idea was to have a significant instructional component. Professor Philip Korth was the first faculty coordinator, and various faculty helped the instructional program in writing and other areas. By now OSS operated its own orientation course on a noncredit basis, and this was also offered to students who enrolled in SUPER. SUPER initially provided 80 students with a structured residential experience and an intensive academic program designed to strengthen their preparation in written and oral communication, mathematics, and science, and to ease their adjustment to university life.

This program, too, succeeded in fostering a greater involvement of the students with the faculty and in the university. The funding from the Office of Minority Equity continued for another year, and then Michigan State assumed full responsibility. The full funding of SUPER by MSU came because of recommendations contained in a report to the provost from the Supportive Services Advisory Committee in 1989 and from a similar proposal contained in the first MSU IDEA (Institutional Diversity: Excellence in Action). SUPER has remained under OSS and operates there quite successfully. The SUPER, SROP, and McNair programs have built collaborative linkages between OSS staff and faculty in selected departments across the university.

Despite these major accomplishments, there has not been recognition of efforts to expand MSU's outreach to minority communities across the state. College Day continues to be the university's largest outreach program to minority communities. We obtained funding for this initiative from the Michigan Office of Minority Equity. Later, we doubled the effort when Pamela Bellamy, an African American woman in my area, developed a proposal for a Talent Search program funded by the U.S. Department of Education. Each year these programs reach thousands of African American, Hispanic, Asian-American, Native American, and white students from high schools across the state. There is no support provided for this effort by the Kellogg Foundation grant that funded Lifelong Education Programs and outreach activities at MSU.

▼   ▼   ▼

During summer 1986 I spent four weeks at Harvard University's IEM program. I also encouraged Lonnie Eiland to apply for the two-week seminar at Harvard. Lonnie earlier had been appointed by me as director of the Undergraduate University Division. I arranged accommodations, as did all of those who participated in the Harvard seminar, at the Charles Hotel near the campus. These were superb, although I had to take the president of the University of Guam as a roommate. Of course, we were very, very busy. Harvard IEM managers had provided us with substantial reading material, literally volumes. We addressed such topics as the law and higher education, stress management for academic administrators, marketing and management, data collection and processing methods of higher education, affirmative action, and budgets and accounting procedures. Our final session dealt with leadership. Each week we were assigned to a different group of no more than eight people, each with its own leader, recorder, and group facilitator. This worked .well, particularly rotating people week after week. Over the four-week period we could have significant interactions with at least half of the participants in the IEM. Another feature of the program that impressed me was the use of the Case Study Method and audience participation. The method was new to me, particularly as a chemist. Using it, we read issue papers that discussed in detail some major issue or problem, and we then discussed the case within our groups and within the larger plenary session. It was a fascinating approach, and I would adopt it later and become known for it in the workshops and training programs conducted for MAEOPP and NCEOA.

The Harvard IEM also introduced me to a multiracial group of more than 100 people. As I participated, I wondered why I had not been sent to it earlier in my administrative career. Others had gone, including Fred Carlisle, Connie Stewart, and Moses Turner. (Fred went on to become the provost at Miami University in Ohio and then provost at Virginia Polytechnic.) Connie helped me by writing a letter in support of my nomination to the Harvard IEM.

The Harvard experience was total. The people were very receptive to interaction with one another, which helped to make for a great four weeks. The staff included a recreational program that was most beneficial as well. Sharon Dade was the coordinator for activities at the conference. She has since left the program and moved on to other things, but I think she was the heart and soul of the IEM, and I cannot imagine that it is still the same without her. She showed a great deal of concern for those of us in the program. She had arranged an opportunity for us to be addressed at the Harvard Faculty Club by Derek Bok, the president of Harvard. The president of Wesleyan University spoke at dinner one evening, describing how she dealt with problems that arose when her Board of Trustees would not endorse disinvestment in South Africa, of which she was a strong supporter.

Jesse Jackson visited the Charles while we were there, with an entourage of staff and body guards. He was easy to approach, and I did so, giving him warm greetings and telling him what a pleasure it was to meet him. The next day he gave a major presentation at a reception in the Charles Hotel. Jesse was laying the foundation for his run for the presidency—at least in the primaries—in 1988.

While all of the sessions at the Harvard IEM were impressive, the most moving was one on leadership, near the end of the program, conducted by Dr. Terry Bolman. We had an extensive discussion on the qualities of leadership, and we had even done play acting with different participants taking different roles the day before. The closure of our stay at the IEM was also affecting us as we went through this session. Many of us did not want to leave and return to our individual campuses. You must recall that this was a group diverse in gender, racial/ethnic background, and the characteristics of the institution and region of the country from which we had come. The racial issue had inevitably come up during the conference and had caused some tension. It was in this atmosphere that one morning after our group meetings we assembled in our plenary session, and Terry Bolman (also a manager of the Harvard IEM) informed us that we were to watch a movie of an outstanding leader and were to analyze his speech. This was unexpected, but we watched the film. It included the speech given by Martin Luther King, Jr., during the March on Washington, in front of the Lincoln Memorial, in 1963—one of the greatest speeches ever given, and one of the most moving. I was sitting next to the provost of North Carolina State University, who was moved to tears. I was certainly near tears, and so were most of the 100 plus people. It was not just the speech that reached us, it was a release of tension, it was the speech as the culminating event of what had been for each one of us a memorable experience.

While in Cambridge I took the opportunity to go on a bus tour which included the Kennedy summer home and the coast of Massachusetts. The IEM made arrangements for the entire group to visit the John F. Kennedy Presidential Museum and Library. This was a unique opportunity. We had a full tour, plus a sumptuous meal in the main lobby of the facility, underneath the largest American flag I have ever seen.

I revisited Harvard's IEM for two follow-up sessions; one on assessment and the other on the undergraduate experience (presented by Ernest E. Boyer).

My participation in the Harvard IEM gave me a much broader view of possible options for me in higher education administration. I began to think about becoming president of a university. An opportunity arose in 1989, when I was invited to apply for the position of provost at Prairie View A&M University, near Houston, Texas. This was a fine opportunity, and I visited the campus and had extensive meetings with its president, Percy Pierre, with faculty, and with student groups. I also met the chancellor of the Texas A&M University system. It was an excellent visit, and I was being seriously considered. It was at this time that Percy Pierre stepped down, leaving the presidency open, and the chancellor invited me to apply for that position, too. I did so, but I was not successful. Subsequently, I was a finalist for the presidency of the State University of New York at Westbury, a very different type of institution, and I thought that I had a very good visit with the community board, faculty, and student groups. Another finalist, Dr. Eudora Pettigrew, was named president. She had been on the MSU faculty for several years before becoming assistant provost at the University of Delaware.

By now I knew that I had amyotrophic lateral sclerosis (Lou Gehrig's Disease), and I did not seek additional positions.

▼   ▼   ▼

In 1986 I had already begun reflecting upon David Scott's approach to his position as provost. It became clear to me that the pace would quicken. David involved himself directly with racial/ethnic issues and did not avoid the various minority groups; he wanted to meet directly with them to hear their concerns. At this time the Black Faculty and Administrators Association had been meeting regularly and decided to make several recommendations to the provost. The leader of the BFAA was Ernest Moore, a professor of audiology and speech sciences.

A group of Black deans (and people in similar positions) also began regular breakfast meetings; the membership varied, and Joe Darden, dean of Urban Affairs Programs, tended to take the lead. Lee June attended regularly, as did I. Dean Julia Miller of the College of Human Ecology came when she could. Barbara Ross-Lee, College of Osteopathic Medicine, and Hiram Davis, director of MSU Libraries, attended several times. This working group developed a series of recommendations to the provost in response to proposals made by the Women's Advisory Committee to the Provost. This called for many changes related not only to women but also to minorities at MSU.

We felt it was important to let the provost know our views on this matter, and there was some concern that the BFAA would not move expeditiously enough to develop a coherent and effective response. I volunteered to prepare the draft for us to review. The document called for many changes, both for faculty and administrators and for undergraduate and graduate enrollments. For example, we wanted more African American faculty. There had been some progress in hiring administrators, but the group felt that more was needed. There were serious concerns with the lack of progress in the recruitment, enrollment, and graduation of African Americans at the Ph.D. level, and the paper called for substantially greater efforts. Also addressed was the need for MSU to increase the enrollment of undergraduate African Americans, and concern was expressed about the high percentage of those enrolled in lower division rather than upper division. This paper was delivered to the provost in 1988. There was no immediate response, other than that it had been received and would be studied.

Meanwhile, Provost Scott's agenda began to emerge, including establishment of the Council to Review Undergraduate Education. This would clearly fall in my area, as assistant provost for undergraduate education, and I had already made available to the provost the surveys conducted for me by James McComb and the Social Science Research Bureau. These documented students' serious reservations about aspects of their undergraduate experience, such as the need to take the elementary writing courses offered by the Department of American Thought and Language. Many felt they had already developed that competency in secondary school. There were complaints about the General Education curriculum, which included a year's work in writing or ATL and a year of study in natural science, social science, and the humanities. Faculties devoted exclusively to teaching these courses were located in the respective departments in the colleges of Arts and Letters, Natural Science, and Social Science. As noted earlier, students questioned the quality of mathematics instruction and the use of foreign teaching assistants (particularly in mathematics). They wished to be able to do work in their major much earlier in their study at Michigan State University.

The concerns of faculty about undergraduate education were less clear, at least to central administration. There had been no recent surveys of faculty to determine their opinions. Central administration had several concerns, however—some quite evident and well known, others less so. These issues were fairly common at other major universities across the country and, indeed, were reflected in Ernest E. Boyer's book. There he talked about the undergraduate curriculum and the attention given to the quality of undergraduate teaching. Boyer called for a core curriculum that addressed various areas of knowledge in ways different from what then occurred. For example, from his position at the Carnegie Foundation for the Advancement of Teaching, he saw a nation of universities serving a much, much more diverse student population. He was aware of the demographic trends affecting the nation and various regions, and he saw that the implications for higher education and the undergraduate curriculum would be profound. He vigorously pressed for more diversity in all aspects of the undergraduate curricular experience.

Administrators at MSU felt we had too many faculty committed to general education in the departments of American Thought and Language, Humanities, Natural Science, and Social Science. The state legislature believed we had too many faculty for the undergraduates we served. (Personally, I always considered this ironic, given that MSU enrolled more undergraduates than any other university in the state, and did so every year.) The deans of the colleges of Arts and Letters, Natural Science, and Social Science, along with the provost, wanted the general education departments eliminated. They wanted to move the GE faculty back to the traditional departments within the parent colleges. This was never stated as an explicit goal, but it was there, nonetheless.

Our approach within the Office of the Provost to organizing a committee to review undergraduate education was to decide upon its size and then develop a charge. In this manner, I learned more about how David Scott would approach such matters. He relied heavily upon the staff and made it very clear that he valued what he considered the faculty opinion more than that of administrators on such issues. For example, early on he had named Larry Sommers acting assistant provost for academic administration. Sommers had considerable experience as a member of the faculty and chair of the Department of Geography, and he also had been responsible for a substantial review of International Studies and Programs. Scott would involve Sommers and me with the Council to Review Undergraduate Education (CRUE). At the time we began CRUE, the provost's staff included Associate Provost Lou Anna K. Simon; me; Bob Banks, assistant provost for academic personnel; Larry Sommers; and two administrative fellows—Nancy Pogel and Marcellette Williams—who were faculty members in the departments of American Thought and Language and English, respectively.

We developed a charge for CRUE, which I drafted. I had suggested that Scott model this after the Council on Admissions and Student Body Composition convened years earlier by President Clifton Wharton, but excluding alumni participation. There was also a desire by most of the staff and the provost to keep the committee small. Of course, it had to be broadly representative of the faculty, and we wanted there to be major links with important areas within the governance system. All of that dictated a committee larger than wished but smaller than the Commission on Admissions and Student Body Composition. In the matter of a chairperson, Scott pressed very hard and had good support among the staff for a scholar who would be responsible for delivering a report to him and to the academic community. No one could argue with that, but I went to great lengths to remind the provost that the person chosen also had to be able to manage a large group of people. I thought that was a very important feature. In addition, I advised the provost that his perspective about the written report—that the chairperson would write the report, and that it would "virtually be that person's report"—could be a problem with the faculty on the committee. The report generated by CRUE inevitably would reflect the direct ideas of its members, and they would perceive it as theirs. Finally, the provost selected as chair Dr. Linda Wagner-Martin, a distinguished professor in the Department of English and well respected around the university.

The charge to CRUE was developed over several weeks and reflected the many areas of concern already noted. I suggested to the provost several approaches for getting the committee started and ways in which we might organize their work. On the latter, Viciki Dukelow, my executive assistant, and I developed the idea of using a large three-ring binder with CRUE clearly designated on the cover. That idea had come, in part, from the way we had worked at the Harvard IEM. The binders were a useful way of bringing many pieces of information together. An array of background material had been assembled for the committee to look at before beginning their deliberations. These included the results of surveys of MSU students and information about other universities' efforts to review undergraduate education. This would be the first major review of undergraduate education at MSU in two decades, since the report of the Committee on Undergraduate Education (CUE Report) in 1967.

To help launch CRUE's deliberations, I arranged, with the concurrence of the provost, for Dr. Ernest E. Boyer to visit with us during a kickoff luncheon at Kellogg Center. This was an excellent idea I thought, since I had heard Boyer speak on two occasions at Harvard. It also seemed to me that this was the kind of person with whom Scott needed to have more contact on the national level, as he seemed to have a great deal to say, and people like Boyer could give him a forum for doing it. I contacted Boyer, who was willing to participate.

Boyer talked at length and with emotion about his concerns with quality undergraduate education in U.S. institutions of higher learning. He made a big impact upon the group. He had been provided with background information on general education at MSU, to which he gave brief attention during his remarks.

CRUE began organizing itself under the leadership of the chair. Viciki and I had arranged for the board room to be the location of all the meetings. The council would meet in the evenings over the next year, and I attended most of these sessions, except one period in summer 1987, when I had to attend a conference at Southampton University. Larry Sommers also participated in the meetings, and Provost Scott frequently joined in.

A major opportunity for Scott to address the council and give his perspective on the charge to CRUE occurred during a retreat at the MSU Kellogg Biological Station at Gull Lake, Michigan. Scott talked at length and off the cuff with the council, but unfortunately, no transcript was made. The provost stated that there would be no new money to fund major new initiatives in this area or in other areas in the years ahead, but he did not want the council to be too concerned with this. They were to come up with what they perceived to be the best undergraduate education experience for students at Michigan State. Scott also clearly saw the issue of diversity discussed by Ernest Boyer as having significant implications for whatever undergraduate curriculum emerged from CRUE. The provost also made it very clear that he thought of the university as a community and wished to see that stressed more at MSU, and one way of doing that was to have a new curriculum for all undergraduates that approached much more closely a common core than did the current program. I must note here that Scott did not call for the dissolution of the departments of general education, nor did he rule out their dissolution.

I reported to the provost, usually at the staff meetings, on how the deliberations of the group were proceeding, but there was a period when I had to be absent. I had a prior commitment to take part in a conference on the freshman year experience at Southampton, England. This would be my first international conference on higher education for undergraduates, and I very much looked forward to going. I had also arranged for two additional staff to submit papers, both of which were accepted. These were Florence Harris, OSS director, and Deborah Galvan, her assistant director, who managed tutorial programs.

My wife, Ruth, arranged a trip to England also, so we took our daughter with us for a short vacation while we were there. Unfortunately, the entire family could not go, as Bramlett spent the summer on an internship for a law firm in New York City. Ruth was Visiting Exchange Professor at the Center for Racial and Ethnic Studies at the University of Warwick, about 100 miles from London. I arranged a rental car to get around England, and we made a brief sightseeing journey the first couple of days. At Westminster Abbey, much to our surprise, we came upon Florence Harris and Deborah Galvan, also headed to Southampton. We chatted, took pictures, and then went our separate ways.

The following day I had to take Ruth and Priscilla up to Warwick, an exciting drive. I had rented a small Ford Escort; most of the other cars on the highway were Rolls Royce, Mercedes Benz, and so forth. I discovered that I had to bear left and stay in that left lane, as the traffic moved very fast—a much faster pace than I was willing to risk with my family in a Ford Escort. Furthermore, I did not know the road. But we arrived at Warwick safely. Ruth spent time meeting with faculty, using the library and research facilities, and meeting with West Indian organizations and community activists in Warwick and Birmingham. Within a few hours of our arrival I headed to Southampton, on the southern coast, making a brief stop at Oxford to see the university. I was surprised by the large cooling towers indicative of a nuclear power station so near to town.

I drove on to Southampton, where I joined Florence, Deborah, and the 150 or more participants at this international conference. We had a free day, so I took Deborah and Florence with me on a side trip to Stonehenge, Bath, and the famous Roman excavations. Over the next several days we presented our papers, which were very well received. There were serious concerns in English colleges and universities with the issue of diversity, too, although most of the English representatives were men, not women or minorities. Women also seemed to have a minor role in university administration. In contrast, there was significant diversity among the delegates from the United States.

At the close of the meeting, I returned to the University of Warwick, picked up my wife and daughter, and drove to Cambridge for a day. Then we were off to Dover and the jetfoil to Belgium. There we met with two of Ruth's former graduate students who were residing in Brussels—Eveleyne Lucia and Manuel Lopez. We had a great visit with them, and they invited us to join them later in the south of France. We did, but first we went by train to Paris. Our friends had convinced me of the wisdom of giving up my car. It was simply easier.

We did all the things you expect to do in Paris, visiting the Louvre, Notre Dame, the Champs-Élysées, the Arc de Triomphe, Napoleon's Tomb, and the Eiffel Tower. Priscilla thoroughly enjoyed it. She was particularly happy because of our hotel arrangements. In Brussels we had a common room, which gave Priscilla little privacy, but in Paris I realized immediately the room was too small for the three of us. I asked the hotel clerk if we could get another room for my daughter. She gave us the key to the adjacent room, and I later learned she charged us for one room only. Contrary to what others have experienced, we found the people of Paris to be thoroughly delightful. We took Priscilla out to visit Versailles, which was being restored by the French government. That was a beautiful side trip, if only to see the magnificent gardens surrounding this enormous palace.

From Paris we went to Avignon by TGV, the fast train. With Priscilla's knowledge of French, and my wife's knowledge, we could talk with people at the train stations while we were in Belgium and France. The TGV was indeed fast and comfortable. We were met at Avignon by Evelyne and Manuel and taken to their family's home in l'Orange, a large chateau. We stayed there for three nights, touring the vineyards and the Roman ruins in the area, including the Roman theater still being used. Priscilla, again, was getting quite an extensive exposure to French culture and surely benefiting in ways that I could not, since I had studied neither French nor the culture. The family was very gracious, and we most appreciated it. We attended a wine festival at the city of Château Neuf du Pape and had a chance to see the parade and the many displays. I also did a bit of wine tasting as I went through the area.

From Avignon we traveled by train to Venice, where we took the obligatory gondola ride and visited the glass blowers at Marino, where we made a purchase. Then we spent several days in Florence, viewing the many art treasures in this great city. We saw Michelangelo's *David* and many other works of art. From Florence we continued to Rome, with its many fascinating sights, and from there returned to the United States.

It had been a great trip for each of us, although it did take me away from the CRUE deliberations. I would learn that Larry Sommers had brought some hard issues before this body.

▼   ▼   ▼

Discussions by CRUE of the curriculum for undergraduates had focused on general education from the outset. The council did not as a matter of principle discuss general education with the view to evaluating its overall effectiveness. Instead, it went immediately to the development of a new curriculum that reflected the content and philosophy as espoused by the provost and by Ernest Boyer, but appropriate to MSU. This curriculum inevitably and necessarily raised the question of the status of the existing general education departments, and the council was grappling with this issue when I returned. It would bother the council throughout much of the remainder of its deliberations. Eventually, it arrived at a way of addressing this problem, and it did so before developing the final report to the provost in spring 1988, but this did not come easily or quickly.

In 1987, CRUE's chair, Dr. Linda Wagner-Martin, accepted an endowed professorship at another institution. She agreed to review and help write the final report, but a new chairperson had to be selected. Two co-chairs were chosen—Professor Richard Phillips from the Department of Mathematics, and Professor Jenny Bond from the College of Human Ecology. They worked together effectively and kept CRUE progressing toward completion of its charge. The interactions of the provost with the committee continued as well. A draft report went through many iterations before being adopted and presented to the provost. The council had worked long and hard. It had grappled with the issue of the general education faculty, but in developing a structure for the new core curriculum proposed, it assumed that the curriculum would be taught by any faculty at Michigan State. This left open the question of the general education departments and their role. It was the general assumption that wherever the faculty were finally located, they would have a role—but not the only role—in teaching the new core curriculum, called Integrative Studies.

The council also recommended new entrance and graduation requirements and introduced the idea of diversity to the undergraduate curriculum and to the majors as well. CRUE called, in short, for a full restructuring of the undergraduate curriculum. This was important, because it had been an expectation and hope of the Office of the Provost that CRUE would take a position on an institutional calendar change from quarters to semesters. CRUE merely stated that we should not reformulate the curriculum and then later make a decision on the change in academic calendar; both should be done together. In addition, CRUE had arranged early for a survey of the faculty to obtain their views on undergraduate education. From this emerged the faculty's positive view of a change in the academic calendar from quarters to semesters.

After some considerable discussion in the governance system, the report of the Council to Review Undergraduate Education was accepted by the Academic Council in spring 1988. This was with the understanding that the provost would move ahead, carrying out various recommendations contained in the report, which would flow back through the governance system for review and approval. We were not through yet!

The University Committee on General Education, which was part of the academic governance system, meanwhile, was wondering about what role, if any, it would have when this new curriculum was put in place. The general education departments were very concerned about the CRUE report. The provost and I, with the assistance of the provost's staff and elements of the governance system, developed two papers. One was a commentary from the Office of the Provost on the report itself, and the second addressed implementation of the core curriculum. In the first paper, among other things, the provost rejected the organizational structure for Integrative Studies proposed by CRUE and suggested instead that:

1. there be centers or institutes for Integrative Studies in the colleges of Arts and Letters, Natural Science, and Social Science;
2. the general education departments be dissolved;
3. general education faculty be reassigned to other units within the appropriate college; and
4. the number of required transcollegiate courses be reduced from two to one.

Provost Scott decided, in part at a request from the deans, to meet with the faculties of the general education departments. The meeting with the faculty of the Department of Humanities was well attended and the discussion heated. Scott was not to be turned around on this matter. He held his ground in support of CRUE and his response to the proposal, but he noted that he would consider the points made by the faculty in this discussion with him. A critical concern was the transfer of faculty to a new department. Faculty clearly felt traumatized by this entire experience, which in some cases called upon them to teach a curriculum different from the one they had been hired to teach. One must sympathize with them. We revised the core curriculum implementation memorandum to reflect their concerns regarding the transfer from one department to another.

The transfer of faculty took longer than anticipated and was not completed until well into the 1988-1989 academic year. Meanwhile, we developed a statement of principles to guide the process. Arrangements had to be made with the home department for accepting the general education faculty. Salaries had to be transferred. The role and responsibility of general education faculty had to be spelled out in detail. The statement of principles helped to achieve these ends.

The deans had expressed concern about the role of the proposed Office of Integrative Studies. The deans were not clear about its implications for them as deans, with major responsibility for the undergraduate curriculum. We retained the office with the understanding that the director of the Center for Integrative Studies within each college (Arts and Letters, Natural Science, and Social Science) would have the major responsibility for his/her own components of the curriculum. This would need to be developed in light of what CRUE and the provost had to say about it. The Office of Integrative Studies would have primary responsibility for the development of transcollegiate courses by every college within the university. The colleges went on to staff their respective centers, which were in place by the 1989-1990 academic year. The curriculum at this point did not address the writing component of Integrative Studies. For that the provost appointed a Writing Task

Force and charged it with developing a program consistent with the recommendations of CRUE and CRUE Implementation Memorandum #5.

The Writing Task force deliberated over several months and finally proposed a requirement calling for all undergraduates to complete one writing course. In addition, for students who were less well prepared, a four-credit developmental writing course would be required. Because this was to be writing across the curriculum, not just writing in the first year, the report also called for two courses in writing in the major. The intent here was to have every major require two courses with significant writing content. The report stipulated additional requirements for Honors students. Clearly, this was a significant departure from the current writing program. The net effect would be, if implemented, that students who entered MSU with good or excellent writing skills could qualify for the regular tier one writing course and would have fewer contact hours in writing in their first year than they did under the quarter system. Students needing assistance would have additional contact hours, above and beyond those required in the current remedial sequence. This was a reasonable proposal, but there was discontent within the Office of the Provost and the governance system. The report did not explain well enough the criteria to be used in evaluating students in writing courses, nor did it specify the content of these courses. We later learned that the Department of American Thought and Language faculty wanted to offer the same array of courses that they currently offered. Eventually, a revised writing group developed a report that retained the essentials but was more explicit about grading criteria, the Honors requirement, and other matters.

▼   ▼   ▼

In 1988 the University of South Carolina held the Second International Freshman Year Experience Conference, this time at Cambridge University. In addition, a preconference activity for a limited number of people would be held at Oxford University.

Lonnie Eiland, director of the Undergraduate University Division, attended both conferences with me. I found the week-long workshop at Oxford particularly helpful. The focus was on getting faculty to improve instruction and using the freshman year experience course as a vehicle for achieving that. The basic idea was to train faculty to handle the assignment and encourage them to experiment with different instructional models that required class participation. There I learned how the University of South Carolina had involved faculty in designing their Freshman Year Experience course, which was used to get to know the students and to develop and use new instructional techniques. I felt that this approach could be very useful at MSU and was convinced that we should develop and set up a Freshman Year Experience course or courses. From Oxford I went on to Cambridge for the main conference, where I also learned a great deal.

While in Cambridge I had an opportunity to go punting on the Cam with a small group of people from different parts of the world with whom I had spent the week at Oxford. It was an enjoyable experience, on a beautiful day; the punter stood at the rear, barefoot (usually), pushing our boat downstream with the long pole. It was very restful and relaxing. I can recall our opening a bottle of wine and sharing cups around in our boat, sipping Chardonnay as we moved slowly along.

I also had an opportunity to take a side trip to visit Bob Fiore and his Spanish class at the University of Denia, Spain. That was a thoroughly enjoyable experience, in no small measure because my son, Bramlett, was taking classes at the university. We traveled all around Denia and ate some of the most delicious seafood I have ever had—all freshly caught in the Mediterranean by Spanish fishermen. From there I returned home, as events at Michigan State commanded my attention.

▼   ▼   ▼

At the beginning of the 1988-1989 academic year I had initiated a survey of undergraduates at MSU. The Social Science Research

Bureau, now the Center for Survey Research within the Institute for Public Policy and Social Research, conducted the survey on a random sample, stratified by race and gender. Telephone interviews were a critical part of the exercise. This approach had proved quite effective in other surveys conducted by the bureau. Our goal was, in part, to prepare a data base so that in the future we could go back and reassess the same students, or at least some of them. (The survey involved first-year students through seniors.) The results would not come out until spring 1989, and by that time there was serious trouble on campus.

Jeffrey Robinson, the head of the Student Chapter of the NAACP, had made a major complaint to the administration about racism at the school. The charge was broadly discussed within the university community. Soon enough, Reverend Loyce Lester, claiming to represent a parent group in Detroit, joined the crisis with a letter to the president expressing concerns about the treatment that our African American students were receiving. Reverend Lester was an important community leader in Detroit and had led various boycotts in the past. Eventually, he demanded a meeting with President DiBiaggio.

The provost's group became a think tank of sorts for David Scott across the next several months. We had never had a major parent protest at Michigan State in my 25 years on the campus. I do not know the background leading up to the meeting, but I do know that somewhere in the process Trustee Joel Ferguson had a role. A meeting was scheduled in the board room between the president and Reverend Lester and representatives of the parent group. This was a surprise to me, but I managed to arrange my schedule so that I could be present. The meeting preludes were a circus. Outside the Administration Building the press and camera crews had gathered with remote transmission equipment, and they joined the parents group on the elevators, Reverend Lester in the lead. Clearly, President DiBiaggio was not expecting this kind of gathering. He looked quite surprised, disturbed, and concerned; I had never seen him this way before. Reverend Lester wanted the press to participate or at least be present during the meeting, but this was clearly unacceptable. Enter Trustee Joel Ferguson, who excluded the press and TV cameras. With those ground rules, the meeting went on in a full board room.

I was sitting next to a man I did not know but who I assumed was with the parents group. The president was at the head of the table, as was Reverend Lester. President DiBiaggio welcomed the visitors to the university, expressing his personal concern at the circumstances that had brought them to this moment. As he was about to continue, Reverend Lester interrupted and read from a prepared statement. Eventually, the meeting settled down to a point at which some of the parents could address the group. Meanwhile, Provost David Scott had returned from out of town and joined the meeting, sitting at the end of the table opposite the president. I expect that David had never seen a confrontation such as this in his life. It was a quite unsettling meeting, and one from which the president needed extrication. Later, the man sitting next to me began to address the president. He was much more direct, firm, and challenging in his communications. It was at this point that David Scott tried to intervene. The man next to me demanded to know who David was, and David identified himself as provost. This had no effect on the speaker, who advised David to sit and be quiet, that he was interested in talking with the president, not with any of his subordinates. David insisted upon being included and was subsequently invited to leave. I later learned that this man was Dr. Cloyzelle K. Jones, the president of the National Urban Coalition, with which Reverend Lester was also involved. We were clearly dealing here with a community activist of the first order. Cloyzelle Jones was a sharp contrast with Reverend Lester, who was very "hip" in the way he dressed and wore his hair. Whatever his appearance, Reverend Lester was accepted by the group he represented and seemingly had a parental relationship to the student, Jeffrey Robinson, who had made the original complaints of racism. The meeting concluded with the understanding that there would be further communication between the president and the group, and that there would be an explicit effort at the university to address the racism that had so negatively affected students.

There followed some communications between the MSU Black Faculty and Administrators Association (BFAA) and Reverend

Lester, and a small group of African American faculty visited his church in Detroit one Sunday morning. There we heard parents' complaints about the treatment of their sons and daughters at Michigan State. They did not hold us accountable for these experiences, but on the contrary were pleased that we had come to listen to their concerns. This problem of racism became a continuing item of discussion within the BFAA. Eventually, the president agreed to establish the Citizens Advisory Committee, with which he met regularly. The committee was charged to address issues of diversity within the university community and provide advice and counsel to the president and members of his immediate staff.

In the middle of this controversy my survey results became available, and after discussion with the provost I released the report to the press. The survey had raised a range of questions about students' experiences at Michigan State. For example, we learned that students studied differently depending upon their racial/ethnic background. Whites and African Americans tended to study alone and to interact less with others. Hispanics and Asian Americans tended to study in groups, but with students different from their own racial/ethnic group. But the interest of the press was not in this aspect of the survey. We had asked one question about the extent to which students experienced racist incidents at Michigan State University. The responses varied by racial/ethnic group. We only took a positive response as indicative of reality if the student followed that up by describing the racial incident. It turned out that incidents were reported by all racial/ethnic groups, but usually they involved African Americans and whites. Thus, the survey results tended to confirm the experiences of Jeffrey Robinson and other students who had reported being the victims of such incidents. This hit the press over the Easter weekend. My wife and I were at the Palmer House in Chicago when I received a telephone call from a radio station in Detroit. They asked about the report and asked me to talk to another caller, Jeffrey Robinson. He and I spoke briefly on the telephone and on the radio about my report. We would subsequently interact more, but there were no conflicts between my report and his experiences.

▼   ▼   ▼

This was also the year in which the Supportive Services Advisory Committee (SSAC) delivered its report to the provost. Work had begun a year earlier, when the committee decided it was time to give the provost some advice and counsel regarding the direction of the programs and the establishment of new policies and procedures for support programs at Michigan State. The recommendations, quite unlike those coming from the BFAA to the provost, were much more narrow in their focus. They addressed undergraduate education and academic support programs for undergraduate minority and disadvantaged students at Michigan State. The first section pointed to the need for continued efforts to recruit and enroll undergraduate minority students. An analysis was given of enrollment distribution, by year, of minority and white students for every college within MSU. This was the only report of its kind in the university that had called attention to this aspect of the undergraduate minority and disadvantaged student experience. For example, certain patterns became clear. We already knew that minority students had lower retention rates than white students. What we did not know was that these minority students were distributed quite differently among the colleges within academic classes.

Colleges fell into one of three different categories when examined from this perspective. In one category were colleges that had an even distribution of minority students across years or a low enrollment of undergraduate minority students. Examples were the colleges of Arts and Letters and Education. A second category had minority students clustered in the upper division and white students evenly distributed among each class. A prime example was the College of Agriculture, which had difficulty recruiting students from minority backgrounds as entering freshmen. Most of their minority students gained admission as juniors, after they had been at the university a while and had become aware of opportunities in agriculture they wished to pursue. The third category were the problematic colleges: Business, Engineering, and Natural Science. Many minority students were clustered in the lower division (freshmen and sophomores), and there were substantially smaller numbers in the upper division. This was in contrast to the distribution for white students, which was more even. In these colleges two factors operated. One was that the programs were of great interest to minority students, who eagerly sought them out as entering freshmen; this helped explain the high concentration in the lower division. The second was that the significant quantitative requirement made it difficult for students to continue unless they could handle mathematics successfully; this helped explain the upper division drop off. This report and its recommendations were shared not only with the provost but also with the deans of every college on campus, so that all were aware of the situation as it existed in 1989.

The report made 39 recommendations to the provost. The hope was that he would take steps to remedy the problems identified. It was not expected that this would occur all at once. As it turned out, the provost had also been busy. He had a good impression of the University of Wisconsin's Madison Plan, which had called for significant changes in the way the university addressed the needs of minorities, women, and other groups. David Scott developed a plan responsive to the needs of Michigan State, the MSU IDEA (Institutional Diversity: Excellence in Action). This plan was much broader than that proposed by SSAC or by the BFAA.

One intent of IDEA was to begin to address affirmative action and its implications. It was the feeling that affirmative action had suffered under the Reagan and Bush administrations and would soon be out of vogue. We needed a replacement locally, and IDEA was it. It was modeled after similar programs that had emerged or were emerging at other institutions across the country. There had been frustration with the affirmative action approach from the very beginning, and there was a mounting reaction against it throughout the nation. While MSU faculty and administrators were more diverse than in the 1960s and 1970s, not very much progress had been made. It was not at all clear that the MSU IDEA would be any more successful in altering that reality, and that reality remains unaltered now. African Americans, in particular, remain underrepresented at every level across the university. MSU

IDEA had potential, but there was neither the will nor the wealth to carry out the many proposals within it. A significant problem was that it emerged from the top down and never involved faculty, staff, and students in its development. As a result, one of its major annual activities, the Diversity Conference, was always relatively poorly attended by the MSU community, except by the administrators and staff who designed the program.

MSU IDEA addressed recruitment and retention of faculty, staff, undergraduates, and graduate students. It also called for many fresh approaches to dealing with the diversity of the academic community, that is, differences as reflected in gender, racial/ethnic background, handicapper characteristics, and sexual orientation.

When David Scott met with SSAC, he could point to his MSU IDEA as one way the institution ought to respond. To mention a few points of overlap, the report from SSAC called for the expansion of a summer program of enrollment for minority students that I had established the previous year, by which they were given an extended orientation to the university and its expectations before their first fall term. That recommendation from SSAC had also been picked up in MSU IDEA under the section related to Support Services. This occurred because of my own involvement with the development of the SSAC report and with the provost's group, where MSU IDEA developed. SSAC also had called for increased efforts to bring the enrollment levels of minority students up to the percentage of population of each racial/ethnic minority group in the state. The MSU IDEA also contained such a recommendation, but it called for a level that reflected the percentage graduated from high school each year, irrespective of racial/ethnic background. Provost Scott expressed his appreciation to SSAC for the report and suggested that it would receive continued attention within his office over the next several months.

On May 11, 1989, approximately 200 African American undergraduates at MSU occupied the lobby of the Administration

Building and refused to allow entry to anyone except supporters. The situation derived from the grievances expressed by Jeffrey Robinson and other students. (This sit-in occurred approximately 20 years after the Wilson Hall episode.) Darius Peyton was a spokesperson for the group, a leader within the MSU Black Student Alliance. Brigette Jones, another spokesperson, was executive director of MSU's Office of Black Affairs. The students handled themselves very, very well and received much encouragement from external groups. Before the confrontation was over, it had broadened to include support from CHISPA (Coalition of Hispanic Students for Progressive Action), APASO (Asian Pacific American Student Organization), and NAISO (Native American Indian Student Organization), together with some white students who joined the protesters in the lobby. The students were at first without food and water, but this changed with support from the BFAA, under the leadership of African American faculty members Barbara Ross-Lee and Ernest Moore, who brought provisions regularly.

The incident at MSU had been preceded by demonstrations at other universities in Michigan. The grievances always were similar, namely, concern about new racism against African Americans. Wayne State University and the University of Michigan both had such protests. In fact, students from Wayne State visited with the MSU group, but they were not encouraged to involve themselves. It was at this time that a substantial issue of freedom of speech arose on campuses across the country. Over the next several years, "political correctness" would also evolve in relationship to freedom of speech as conservatives and liberals debated the reemergence of racism and contrasted it to that of the 1960s. Some would claim, particularly conservatives, that African American students today had no experience with racism, that on the contrary they were misusing this label in the modern context. Many others would dramatically disagree.

The provost's group continued to function as the primary think tank for David Scott throughout the demonstration. He participated in the Executive Advisory Committee (EAC, a group consisting of the president, provost, vice presidents, and selected others) and sought to provide such responses as he could to us on the principal issues and to secure our views and advice. For example, early in the demonstration EAC wanted to call the police and evict the students. That was the attitude of the president and at least some, if not all, of his advisory group. This had been the position taken by the president of Stanford University when students occupied his office. I advised against eviction, which had not been adopted at other institutions in Michigan that had experienced sit-ins and because I thought that would greatly inflame the situation. The students were not evicted, but police sealed off the front entrance so that no one could gain permanent entry. But food and health care continued to be provided to the students. The police handled the front doors. Entry to the building was through the side doors, which meant that I had to walk up four flights of stairs to get to my office. This was an inconvenience that we all endured.

Eventually, negotiations began with Trustee Joel Ferguson, Tom Gunnings, and Ernest Moore (head of the BFAA) trying to act as intermediaries. These led to no major demands in writing from the students. Business went on at the university, and unless one was at the Administration Building, one might have been unaware that a demonstration was taking place. There were counter protests by white students, however, and a long debate about the race baiting that had prompted this entire affair.

It was inevitable that the members of the National Urban Coalition from Detroit, Dr. Cloyzelle Jones and Reverend Loyce Lester, would come forward, express their support, and provide advice to the students. A statement to President DiBiaggio by the group declared solidarity with the students.

At a formal reception in Kellogg Center I had an opportunity to meet with the provost, the president, and others directly involved in handling negotiations with the students, and now with Cloyzelle Jones and Loyce Lester. I quietly took the president aside and recommended that an official negotiator be involved. I suggested Sam Baker from the Office of Personnel, who had formal experience. Subsequently, Baker joined the negotiating team. Later, we received from the students a list of their demands. (The students typed it on a microcomputer belonging to Delores Reed in my office. Apparently, they had no printer for their small portable computer, and they wanted to use the office of someone they could trust.) Once the president received the demands, he compared them with commitments already made in other contexts, such as MSU IDEA. The president sent a formal response based, in part, on materials from the Office of the Provost. Finally, the students gave up occupation of the building and returned to regular academic work.

As had been agreed by the president and the students, the administration sent a statement to the university giving details of the settlement. The memorandum noted that none of the students who had participated in the sit-in were to be disadvantaged by their absence from class during that week-long period. Thus ended the second major African American student demonstration during my tenure at Michigan State.

The effects would continue to be felt well into the 1990s. As a direct result, the president established the statewide Citizens Advisory Committee. In addition, an annual conference on diversity began at Michigan State in 1990. The students had also called for tenure for three African Americans: Moses Turner, vice president for student affairs and services; Ralph Bonner, director of the Office of Human Relations; and Curtis Stokes, a faculty member in James Madison College. The students also recommended that the provost appoint a senior advisor on racial, ethnic, and multicultural affairs. That, too, was subsequently done. It was a full experience for all those involved. All learned through this experience, and I think that all benefited as well.

Who would have predicted the confluence of (1) demands from the BFAA relating to needs of the African American community at Michigan State; (2) the development and emergence within the Office of the Provost, in part on its own initiative but also in response to the developing issues in the larger community and on campus, of a document such as MSU IDEA; (3) activist protests and expressions from African American students of concerns about racial mistreatment at the hands of white students that led to a meeting between parents of these students and the president of MSU; (4) the development by the Supportive Services Advisory Committee of a report to the provost calling for a reemphasis on recruitment and retention of minority students and recommending ways in which this can be done; and, finally, (5) a major sit-in by African American students supported by all multiethnic student groups at MSU?

Many factors led to all these problems. Not the least of them was the fact that the number of African Americans, Asian Americans, Hispanics, and Native Americans enrolling at MSU had grown significantly, although not as much for some groups as for others. In addition, the student body represented a new generation of young people who had grown up after the civil rights era and the Vietnam War. They lacked any personal recollection of the issues that affected generations in the 1960s and 1970s. The educational system had not prepared them well for life on a university campus, where they would be required to grapple anew with issues of personal and group identity while lacking the educational background to facilitate their effort to "find themselves." As a result, a conflict arose between students and the administration and between minority and white students. The latter had been no better prepared educationally to deal with diversity than had minority students. They were the majority, and they possessed a greater sense of superiority of their own culture over those from minority groups. An exception was made for some Asian Americans, who quite often, but not always, excel even more highly than white students. On the matter of affirmative action I have already commented, and I add that the retreat from that policy continues and probably will mean greater conflict and protest by minorities in the future. One beacon of hope is multiculturalism in the undergraduate curriculum at MSU. I have in mind the Integrative Studies curriculum that has evolved from the Council to Review Undergraduate Education. Through it our undergraduates may become more aware of and more sensitive to issues of cultural difference than were previous generations.

This was a lot to handle, but the university survived due to the good feelings for MSU held by all those concerned—students, faculty, and administrators.

▼   ▼   ▼

In 1989 my daughter, Priscilla, completed Okemos High School. My son also graduated from Michigan State University's James Madison College. Therefore, this was a time of planning for my wife and, to a lesser degree, for me. Earlier in the spring, Priscilla, as a student of Professor Deborah Moriarity of the MSU School of Music, presented a full piano concert in Hart Auditorium in the MSU Music Building. It was a fantastic affair, and many attended. We held a reception for her and her teacher following the recital. This was followed by plans for two graduations. My mother expected to come to Okemos for these events, as did Ruth's brothers Louis, Robert, and Merilus, and Merilus' spouse, Gloria, and their daughters, Mindy and Alaina.

We made plans and hoped for good weather. There was sunshine and warm weather for Priscilla's graduation on the football field outside the high school. Several days earlier she had played Debussy's Claire de Lune at a baccalaureate ceremony at a local Lutheran church. Each of the graduates received a diploma from the high school principal, who we knew well. Priscilla had four great years at Okemos High School. She had become a member of the National Honor Society, serving as president in her senior year. She had continued her piano and had taken up the oboe in the Okemos band and orchestra. She also was active in the marching band with the flag corps, and she found the time to play varsity tennis and serve as homecoming queen. With a wide range of colleges to pick from, she chose Stanford.

Bramlett was, of course, quite excited about his graduation, as were we. This would be our first college graduate. Bramlett was in the Honors College throughout his four years and had made many friends. He did not continue with his saxophone while in college, which I regret, but he will return to it someday. He had decided to pursue a degree in international relations and Spanish, encouraged by Professor Robert Fiore. Michael Schechter, a professor in James Madison College who had also taken on duties as assistant dean of International Studies and Programs at MSU, served as his major advisor. Bramlett benefited greatly from such mentors.

Bramlett's graduation ceremonies were in the Great Hall of the Clifton and Dolores Wharton Center for the Performing Arts. As usual, it was well decorated with flowers and plants. The acting dean, Bob Banks, who was also assistant provost for academic personnel, presided. Professor Ken Waltzer gave the main speech. I participated in the ceremony and marched in with the platform party after all the graduates had entered. Since I sat on the stage, I had a perfect view of all Bramlett's guests in the audience. When Bramlett came across the stage, Bob Banks invited me to present the degree. I shall always remember and cherish that occasion.

It is not often that you have two graduates in the same year, and both going off to the same school—Bramlett had been accepted into Stanford Law School. We wished them well and looked forward to the next several years.

▼

CHAPTER TEN

MICHIGAN STATE UNIVERSITY, 1989-1993, & MY YEARS WITH AMYOTROPHIC LATERAL SCLEROSIS

O n an airplane flight to do consulting, I tried in vain to swing my luggage into the compartment above my seat. I felt a great weakness in my right shoulder and almost dropped the bag. Another passenger saw my difficulty and assisted me. That may have been my first indication of the onset of amyotrophic lateral sclerosis (ALS), also known as Lou Gehrig's Disease. Another indication came that winter of 1989. When I went on my usual morning jog at Jenison Field House, I experienced difficulty holding my head up. This continued to bother me when I tried to do work at the computer in my office. I visited a doctor at the MSU clinic, who could not help, and then mentioned my condition to Dr. Ralph Watson, an African American physician in the MSU clinic. I had seen Dr. Watson at a meeting of the MSU BFAA. He urged me to visit him at the clinic, which I did right away, and he told me after the examination that there were several possibilities, including ALS. He wanted me to visit with another doctor in the MSU Clinic, George Ristow, to get further insight. I did not do so immediately, as I had scheduled a trip to Los Angeles to give a workshop for the National Council of Educational Opportunity Associations (NCEOA).

Upon my return, I saw Dr. Ristow, who had me take a series of tests at the Ingham County Medical Facility, where it was determined that I had a neuromuscular disorder that was affecting both my upper and lower extremities. Following other tests, including examinations via nuclear magnetic resonance at MSU, Dr. Ristow gave me a preliminary diagnosis of ALS. This was in late 1989. Up to this point I had not been as candid as I could have been with Ruth and others about my condition, but now I did become concerned. At Dr. Ristow's advice I made contact with the Muscular Dystrophy Association in Lansing to get additional information about services they provided to people with ALS.

I also made use of the Medline Information in the MSU Library. There I reviewed a large number of abstracts about this diseased called ALS. They confirmed what I had heard from my physicians, and they documented the lack of progress being made in research on the causes of the disease. Throughout 1989 and all the way up to 1991, I continued to carry out my duties and responsibilities as assistant provost for undergraduate education and professor of chemistry. By now I regularly wore a neck brace, but I could speak clearly. I delivered my lectures in chemistry, and I did workshops around the country for NCEOA.

ALS did not stop me from continuing to work in the Office of the Provost, but I did make a decision to bring our programs together. I placed the Office of Supportive Services, Office of Programs for Handicapper Students, Upward Bound, the Foreign Teaching Assistant Orientation Program, and the Martin Luther King-Cesar Chavez-Rosa Parks College Day Program under Dr. Lonnie Eiland, director of the Undergraduate University Division (UUD). He understood that I would continue to function as the dean and assistant provost, but his unit would have budgetary responsibility for this new organization. I had two purposes. I wanted to put all of our support programs under one administration and identify a common space for those programs. In addition, I wanted to provide some protection for UUD, which might be vulnerable to elimination in another budget crunch. To ease the management of this new organization, I added an administrative assistant to handle budget for the director of UUD.

Lonnie and I moved ahead with plans to move the Office of Supportive Services and the other units to Bessey Hall so that they could all be near UUD. It turned out we could not do this immediately. The full-scale plans had nonetheless been put together by

Lonnie. We ultimately moved OSS from Erickson Hall to the second floor of Bessey Hall, across from the Learning Resources Center. I hoped that this would result in greater sharing and collaboration between the directors and their staffs, and lead at some point to the merger of the two units.

Meanwhile, the programs in supportive services continued to move along. The SROP and McNair programs had worked quite well together, and by now some students from HBCUs were coming to MSU to participate in summer research. Mary Lee Vance continued to direct the program. The Summer Undergraduate Program Encouraging Retention (SUPER) had also done well, and we had documented evidence of its beneficial effects. Interviews with these students revealed that it helped to ease their transition into Michigan State. They felt they learned the campus in advance of other students and "knew the lay of the land." Having had an opportunity to participate in small classes in the summer, they also felt more comfortable with faculty. SUPER needed to stay. I needed funding to expand it to an enrollment of more than 300 College Achievement Admission Program students.

The Undergraduate University Division, as the home for all of the support programs, seemed a good idea, but I could tell that Florence Harris, director of supportive services, and the other directors would have difficulty working in that context. To the credit of Florence, Judy, and Glenda, they gave it a try. Nonetheless, I heard complaints off and on about problems with the new arrangement, most because UUD staff could not change their thinking and accept the support programs. Perhaps that was too much to expect. I did not reverse my views and rearrange the programs. I left the units under the director of UUD and worked throughout the remainder of 1989 and into 1990 and 1991 to make the plan work. I had high hopes that we would break through to a new working relationship in these units.

In 1989 David Scott had begun to discuss possible changes in the Office of the Provost. At one of these meetings he mentioned his desire to have Barbara Steidle, who was then dean of James Madison College, become assistant provost for academic services. That appointment was made in 1990. To my great surprise the provost removed from my responsibility the Office of Admissions and Scholarships, which had reported to me for ten years. I suppose, in part because I knew then that I had ALS, I did not express a major objection. In any case, Barbara joined the staff and provided some additional assistance in developing a revised writing program, to which I referred earlier. I and a number of faculty had spent several months developing a new writing program along the lines cited in the CRUE report, but this was deemed unacceptable by the provost and others, and Barbara was charged to work with another group to develop a writing program. Ultimately, the one put in place reflected CRUE and the desires of the faculty in the Department of American Thought and Language, who would teach those writing courses.

Meanwhile, ALS continued to work its way with me. I regularly went to the Muscular Dystrophy Association clinic at MSU. I had not yet informed people at work that I had the disease, but as it began to affect my arms and my neck, I did talk with the staff and the provost. I continued my work, however, as ALS did not affect my mind, and I could carry out my responsibilities. I also informed the leadership of NCEOA, MAEOPP, and the American Association for the Advancement of Science. These organizations included people with whom I had worked over many years. Later, in spring 1990, MAEOPP sponsored a recognition program for me in Chicago, in conjunction with the annual spring meeting. I was deeply moved by the many comments made by my colleagues in the association and by others in attendance, from MSU and elsewhere. I received several awards at this program. They included one from the Michigan Chapter of MAEOPP, presented by the chapter president and Florence Harris, director of the Office of Supportive Services at MSU. This plaque recognized my many contributions to MI/MAEOPP. An award from NCEOA and presented by Arnold Mitchem, Executive Director, recognized my exceptional leadership contribution as a founder, visionary, activist, and mentor to NCEOA. Finally, two awards by MAEOPP were an honorary life membership in the association and the establishment of a research scholar excellence award to be given annually in my name. This moment for MAEOPP and for me brought together the membership and provided an opportunity to renew our commitment, remember our past, and renew our fellowship. A number of friends and relatives attended, including my mother, Aunt Cara, Aunt Morabelle, Uncle James, my cousin Katherine Stafford, Aunt Sarah, my cousins Jenola and Maurice, and my friends Frank and Sylvia Nix. I feel that many people—family, friends, and associates at MSU—had a great role to play in generating that idea and in bringing all those people together, with whom I had worked 20 years earlier to help establish the MAEOPP and NCEOA. It was a great occasion.

In 1990 the provost, on my recommendation, appointed John Greene as director of the Office of Integrative Studies. John had responsibility for implementing the transcollegiate course component of the core curriculum. In that respect he would have to work with deans of colleges from across the university, and with an advisory committee of faculty that included the directors of integrative studies in the colleges of Arts and Letters, Natural Science, and Social Science (professors Alan Fisher, F. William Cambray, and Philip Smith). These three directors had already set out the basic outline of the courses that would be developed for the core program. This was yet to be done for the transcollegiate courses, but we had prepared a set of guidelines that flowed from material developed within the Council of Deans under the leadership of Frank Hoppensteadt.

John Greene began to meet his responsibilities using funds made available by me and Associate Provost Lou Anna K. Simon. He hired a secretary and went to work in Kedzie Hall. He was meticulous and thorough in his approach to his new responsibility.

The rest of the core program also moved along. We encountered additional problems with the writing program because of strong feelings in the provost's staff that students should take the same writing course and not have a potpourri of courses from which to choose. The Department of American Thought and Language, whose faculty would have responsibility for the writing program, felt quite differently. They, like all university faculty, were in the midst of preparing for a transition from quarters to semesters. It was their intent to use the same basic courses in the semester system that they had used in the quarter system. They fought hard for this, and in the short term it appeared they had won. That component of the writing curriculum received approval by the University Curriculum Committee and by the Academic Council.

CRUE had also intended that we revise the governance system to give more visibility within its standing committees to the undergraduate component of the curriculum. They proposed dissolving the University Committee on General Education and modifying the University Curriculum Committee by setting up the University Undergraduate Council, with responsibility for the undergraduate curriculum as well as undergraduate policy matters. I was quite excited about this parallel to the Graduate Council. As assistant provost for undergraduate education I would work with the new council. The Graduate Council then would assume similar responsibilities in the graduate sphere, although its size might need to be increased. That plan also would have eliminated the University Committee on Academic Policy, which at the time addressed both undergraduate and graduate policy matters. The only component of the plan ever implemented was the dissolution of the University Committee on General Education.

▼　　▼　　▼

During this period a new African American student group—called As One—emerged at MSU. While the membership was not exclusively Black Muslims, there was a strong representation in that organization. Ezra Hyland, the advisor to the group in the early 1990s, was on the staff of the Office of Supportive Services. As One appeared to have a large base among African American students, although not all supported the group. A real problem arose when As One decided to invite Minister Farrakhan to speak at MSU. (Neither As One nor the provost knew that he had visited MSU years earlier, during the tenure of President Wharton.)

The group sought funding from the Office of the Provost, and some was provided, although it was not specified whether the funds were for Minister Farrakhan's visit. Once the news spread, the Jewish community at MSU and the off-campus Hillel Foundation protested on the ground that antisemitic comments had been attributed to Minister Farrakhan. The era of defense of free speech at MSU and "political correctness" had dawned.

The provost received criticism for his support of As One from several quarters. To his credit, in the name of academic freedom, he did not back down. The visit occurred, and many students turned out, mostly African Americans. Jewish students and community representatives picketed outside the auditorium.

The interest of African American students in individuals like Minister Farrakhan and Stokely Carmichael, who visited later, and a number of other more militant African American leaders is an interesting phenomenon to me. I believe today's African American students view the racial experience more like that in the 1960s, when Black Power was in vogue, but they lack the experience, insight, and commitment of the earlier generation.

Meanwhile, conflicts arose in central administration over the appointment of an athletic director, which received wide publicity in the media. George Perles, the football coach, wanted to be athletic director, too. President DiBiaggio did not feel he should occupy both positions. Eventually, the Board of Trustees appointed Perles athletic director for one year, allowing him to remain as coach, while a national search began for a permanent director. Perles became a candidate. The provost evaluated Perles as athletic director, as required by the Board of Trustees, and gave him a good review, but the Search Committee still felt the two jobs should be separate. In fact, DiBiaggio ultimately appointed Merrily Dean Baker, a white woman, as athletic director; this action caused problems within the African American community, which wanted the African American associate athletic director to be chosen. There were formal protests to the Board of Trustees by African American students, faculty, staff, and members of the Alumni Association.

▼   ▼   ▼

In summer 1989 I traveled to San Jose, Costa Rica with my wife and several of her graduate students to attend a conference on the

African Diaspora. Our group included an Afro-Costa Rican woman, an Afro-Panamanian male, an Afro-Brazilian woman, and a woman from India. On this trip I gained greater insight into the kind of research in which my wife was engaged. There were many excellent presentations at the conference, including the one by my Ruth.

Our group then boarded a van and headed to the City of Limon, on the Atlantic coast. The diverse population includes Asians as well as Afro-Costa Ricans originally from the West Indies, who speak English and Spanish. The research team made trips to outlying areas, and when we returned to San Jose, a landslide that had blocked our passage on the way down had been cleared. It was late at night, so we did not get to see much of the scenery, but going to Limon it had been quite a different story. Costa Rica is a most beautiful country of rolling hills, tropical forests, and plantations of bananas, coffee, and other crops.

The following day we boarded our van for a trip to the Pacific coast, where we visited a number of cities and encountered people of African descent who had obviously been in Costa Rica for a much longer period than those we had met on the Atlantic coast. It was clear they were of African descent, even though most of them did not recognize or acknowledge that. We ended our stay at a resort hotel on the beach, where I went swimming in the Pacific and in the local pool. Our trip back to San Jose was uneventful, but I did see a volcano en route. Our visit was a most interesting experience for me, and both interesting and educational for Ruth's graduate students. One of them would ultimately return to Costa Rica and do a more in-depth study of the people of African descent in that country.

▼   ▼   ▼

In fall 1990 and winter 1991 I continued to struggle with the effects of amyotrophic lateral sclerosis. The disease had begun in my shoulder and neck muscles, which it now affected to a greater extent, and it had progressed to my right arm and was causing me some mobility difficulty, although I could walk. The greatest effect was on my breathing. I received supplemental oxygen at night, because shortness of breath made sleeping difficult. By spring 1991 my need for oxygen had increased, and I could not walk. I had access to a manual wheelchair, and Ruth took me everywhere. My breathing became so difficult that I entered Sparrow Hospital for seven weeks, where I underwent a tracheotomy, was fitted with a "trach," and received a ventilator to assist me in breathing. I left the hospital and returned home to a totally different environment in our family room, created for me by Ruth.

While in the hospital I became quite concerned about my responsibilities at the university and decided to write a letter to Provost Scott resigning as assistant provost for undergraduate education, but retaining my status as a professor of chemistry. This seemed the appropriate thing to do; it took me out of executive management but retained for me the benefits I had accrued in that status. David accepted my resignation but reappointed me consultant to the provost.

I had ordered an electric wheelchair and began operating from that. I returned to work and assumed my new as well as former responsibilities as assistant provost for undergraduate education (no one had been appointed to that position). Delores Reed and I worked together over the next several months to manage the budget until a new administrator was named.

The budgetary situation had not improved during my absence from the campus. The provost, associate provost, and deans were quite preoccupied with planning for the 1992-93 fiscal year. In the meantime, I met with Provost Scott to discuss the units under my responsibility and what I thought should be done with them.

I developed a rather extended paper on this topic and shared it with the provost, but I stopped short of suggesting what should happen at the level of the assistant provost or dean for these programs or units. Following a discussion of this paper, Provost Scott developed his own plan of reorganization for the Office of the Provost. I further occupied myself with planning a conference on retention to be sponsored by the CIC (the consortium of the Big Ten and the University of Chicago), with Pennsylvania State University also invited to participate. Based on data from the previous conference, I planned to have each institution submit a paper describing its retention programs for undergraduates. It was understood by all that the focus would be on minority students.

Every institution responded to the request for papers. Several people from MSU were invited to participate, including Dr. Lonnie Eiland, director, Undergraduate University Division; Dr. Lee June, senior advisor to the provost for Student Academic Support Services and Racial, Ethnic and Multicultural Issues; Dr. Barbara C. Steidle, assistant provost for Academic Affairs; Dr. Elaine Cherney, director, Learning Resources Center; and Dr. Charles Wilson, assistant director of Intercollegiate Athletics. We also invited any deans and members of the provost's staff who wished to participate to attend.

Groups of 8 to 10 participants met together throughout the conference to discuss issues related to retention and strategies for addressing them. We also identified group leaders, group facilitators, and group recorders and defined their functions. Viciki Dukelow assisted in organizing the entire conference and in getting material from each of the institutions. The conference was held February 23-25, 1992, at the Kellogg Center. This was the first conference on retention ever convened by the CIC, and it was appreciated by all those in attendance, as was shown by the conference evaluations. Proceedings of the conference were issued to all participants. The recommendations were as follows:

1. The commitment to quality undergraduate instruction on our campuses should be increased by the better training and/or reorientation of our faculty to the importance of quality teaching, by the better training of teaching assistants (whether foreign or domestic), and by the implementation of appropriate recognition and rewards for quality teaching at every level within the institution.
2. Faculty have historically designed academic support programs, for example, recitation sections associated with large lectures, and we see them reemerging to focus their attention on this area. These faculty should receive the support of their academic units and other administrators.

3. Academic support programs on our campuses should be more regularly evaluated to determine their relative effectiveness. The procedure should be the same as for academic units: evaluations at least every five years by both internal and external evaluators.
4. CIC institutions should gather information on a more systematic basis from undergraduate students who fail to return to the institution as well as from those who remain and earn their degrees.
5. Within the CIC universities, collaboration and interaction between academic support units and colleges, departments, and schools and between faculty and academic support staff must be improved. Academic support programs should place a greater emphasis upon orienting students to the academic life of the institution.
6. There should be more sharing across CIC institutions of data on retention and on academic support programs that are successful.

During this extended period of preparation and implementation of the CIC conference on retention, Provost Scott had developed his reorganization plan. He shared it with me in advance, and I provided him with some additional advice. For example, I suggested that someone in his office should have "undergraduate education" in their title, given its importance to MSU's mission. The provost took responsibilities that I had formerly assumed and distributed them among four different units—the Office of the Provost, the Graduate School, the Office of the Assistant Provost for Academic Services, and the Office of the Senior Advisor to the Provost for Racial, Ethnic, and Multicultural Issues. I will not go into detail here, except to note that all academic support units went to the newly created position of assistant provost for student academic support services and racial, ethnic, and multicultural issues (Lee June).

The academic support programs included the UUD undergraduate academic advising and progress monitoring units, the offices of Supportive Services and Programs for Handicapper Students and the federal programs, Upward Bound, the Martin Luther King, Jr.—Cesar Chavez-Rosa Parks College Day Program, and the Talent

Search Program. (Dr. Pamela Bellamy had, with my support and that of Lonnie Eiland, written a proposal to the U.S. Department of Education for a Talent Search Program. It received funding in 1991, and I placed it and the College Day Program under Dr. Bellamy's direction, with the approval of the U.S. Department of Education.) Dr. Barbara Steidle, assistant provost for undergraduate education and academic services, assumed responsibility, jointly with OSS, for the Summer Undergraduate Program Encouraging Retention as well as for the evaluation and testing program in UUD, Aerospace Studies, Military Science, and the Office of Integrative Studies. The Graduate School, which as yet did not have a dean, assumed responsibility jointly with OSS for the Summer Research Opportunity Program and jointly with Dr. Steidle's office for the Foreign Teaching Assistant Orientation Program. The reorganization was made public through a news release shared with the MSU campus newspaper. The assistant provosts had the authority to reorganize as each saw fit the units assigned to them.

This reorganization led to the placement of all programs for minorities and handicappers under Lee June, an African American male. The other major programs went to Barbara Steidle, a white female, and to the Graduate School. These were largely mainline programs within the university, such as Integrative Studies and the Foreign Teaching Assistant Orientation Program. I thought this was an unfortunate development. During my years in the Office of the Provost I had been responsible not only for support programs for minorities and handicappers but also for programs affecting undergraduates across the entire university, including admissions. That had been quite important to me.

Shortly after this reorganization the BFAA requested and obtained a meeting with four members of the Board of Trustees and with President DiBiaggio and Provost Scott. Tom Gunnings, a member of BFAA and a professor of psychiatry, invited me to attend. Apparently, a previous series of meetings between the provost and the BFAA had not gone well in the view of those present, and at this meeting the BFAA attacked Provost Scott. They noted that none of the mainline university programs—such as the

Honors College, Military Science, and Aerospace Studies—had gone to Lee June. They noted that under this administration there were no African Americans serving as department chairs.

Meanwhile, the Board of Trustees refused to give President DiBiaggio the extension to his contract that he wanted, and subsiquently the president resigned. He went on to assume the presidency of Tufts University effective September 1, 1992 terminating his relationship with MSU effective August of that year. The resignation caught everyone by surprise and created instability within the university at a time of momentous change. A difficult fiscal situation in the state had resulted in decreased support for MSU, and the provost and deans had discussed budget reductions. The university also had decided to change its academic calendar from quarters to semesters, effective September 1992. A new Student Information System would begin with the calendar change, although elements had been put in place earlier. Of course, Provost Scott played a major role in all these activities.

John DiBiaggio had assumed the presidency of MSU with the full support of the Board of Trustees. He had been recruited in part because of his perceived success in fund raising and in dealing with the legislature while president of the University of Connecticut. An outgoing individual, he had mounted a major fund-raising campaign that brought more than $210 million to MSU. Ten million dollars came as a grant from the Kellogg Foundation to fund lifelong education, and two other large sums came from benefactors for building a new addition to the College of Business and to fund a major program to improve teaching in the public schools.

President DiBiaggio had gotten off to a quick start at MSU, especially after he named David Scott as provost. Although the president talked about the land-grant tradition, more than had been the case for his predecessor, he was among those who wanted to make MSU a more highly ranked AAU university. During his tenure, explicit comparisons to other ranked AAU and AAU land-grant universities found MSU wanting. Continuous efforts to obtain more state funding did not succeed. Review and modification of the entire undergraduate curriculum did succeed. The general education program, formerly housed in the departments within the core colleges, was eliminated and replaced with the Integrative Studies Program. Higher admission and graduation requirements were adopted. MSU shifted from quarters to semesters, which gave it a calendar similar to that of the University of Michigan. These changes would forever alter the life of undergraduates, graduates, and faculty at MSU.

The semester system made new demands on students and faculty and enrollment declined. The latter was attributable, in part, to the fact that most courses in the semester system became three-credit courses. When students took their usual four courses, their credit load now averaged twelve hours, rather than the fourteen or fifteen hours carried in the quarter system.

The DiBiaggio years also produced a major review of graduate education and research, resulting in a report called CORRAGE (Council on Review of Research and Graduate Education). It did not have the impact on either the curriculum or research at the graduate level that the CRUE Report had on undergraduate education. This was due in part to the way the committee had been structured and led and in part to the long-standing view at MSU that graduate education and research are matters best left to the faculty and the basic academic units. For example, there was no dean of graduate programs and no vice president for research and graduate studies on staff to interact with this committee on a continuing basis. CORRAGE did make a number of recommendations, including establishment of the Office of Assistant Provost, and Graduate School dean. A new vice president for research and graduate studies would join MSU after the report was completed.

Lifelong education changed in a major way in several steps. The first occurred under the leadership of the dean of the College of Education, who proposed dismantling Continuing Education Programs and restructuring them as Lifelong Education Programs in the colleges. President DiBiaggio approved appointment of a vice provost with responsibility for this area. (Years earlier, MSU had a vice president for continuing education.) Every dean had on the staff an individual responsible for continuing education offerings within that college. Lifelong Education as reconstituted in the 1980s and 1990s placed many more of the resources and responsibilities at the college level, but without the benefit of the coordinators who had carried out the roles before. Under President DiBiaggio there also was an explicit step taken to build a closer relationship between Cooperative Extension Programs and Lifelong Education. The agricultural community was quite angry about this. Eventually, a woman was hired to direct Cooperative Extension Programs, and a new vice provost and dean for agriculture and natural resources—a white male—also was hired. There had been an effort to remove the title of vice provost from the dean of Agriculture and Natural Resources as well as combine Cooperative Extension with Lifelong Education Programs in the new University Outreach effort, but this failed because of resistance from the agricultural community across the state. President DiBiaggio was also responsible for hiring the first woman as director of Intercollegiate Athletics at MSU, or for that matter at any Big Ten university.

In his six-year presidency, John DiBiaggio presided over the greatest number of changes at MSU since the days of John Hannah. He had appointed a great number of new administrators: deans of the colleges of Arts and Letters, Natural Science, Social Science, Agriculture and Natural Resources, Human Medicine, Osteopathic Medicine, Nursing, and James Madison, as well as a provost, general counsel, and vice presidents for research and graduate studies, legal affairs, and governmental relations. Major building projects completed or begun during his tenure included the new Plant and Soil Sciences Building, a remodeling of the Old Horticulture Building, construction and opening of the Breslin Student Events Arena (initiated under President Cecil Mackey), the construction of a new intermural center on the east side of campus, and modifications to campus buildings and grounds to make them even more accessible for handicapper students or more usable by faculty, staff, and students.

On the heels of DiBiaggio's resignation announcement, the university community also had to contend with news that Scott had interviewed for the position of chancellor at the University of Missouri, Columbia. He had agreed to stay on as provost as long as he had at the request of President DiBiaggio. Scott needed to make his own plans and not function under ill-founded assumptions.

Then, in mid-August, he announced that although he had been a finalist for this position, in the spirit of the 1992 Olympics, he had not earned the gold medal but had to settle for silver. He already had informed the staff in early July 1992 that it was his intention to resign as provost and take a leave from the university. Among his reasons, all of which I will not go into here, was the fact he had stayed on at the request of President DiBiaggio, who was now leaving. David announced his official resignation in August. This left the university with nither a president nor a provost during a period of great change. President-designate Gordon Guyer moved quickly to name Lou Anna K. Simon as interim provost on September 2, 1992.

▼   ▼   ▼

In spring 1992, my wife and I prepared for a trip to California to attend Bramlett's graduation from Stanford Law School. It took a great deal of planning, and Ruth handled everything. My illness required that two nurses accompany us to maintain my 24-hour care. We brought along two ventilators (one for backup) and batteries for both my wheelchair and the ventilators. Oxygen was provided by the airline. Supplies needed in California came from a local supplier. Needless to say, it took months to work out the details of this trip. An ALS support group in the Bay Area helped locate an accessible mini-van. My brother-in-law Richard Simms (with whom I stayed, and to whom I will be forever grateful) picked up the van.

The trip went well. The graduation ceremony was outstanding, and we were pleased and proud to be there with our daughter, Priscilla, and other members of the family to see Bramlett walk across the stage and receive his doctor of jurisprudence from Stanford. The occasion brought three of Ruth's brothers together: Richard; Louis, from Lansing, Michigan; and Robert, his wife, Jan, and their granddaughter, Paige, from El Paso and Houston, Texas, respectively.

▼   ▼   ▼

Fall 1992 began the first year at MSU on a semester calendar. This was historic. It was also Gordon Guyer's first year as president-designate and Lou Anna K. Simon's first as interim provost. In addition, Marcellette Williams began a new appointment as assistant to the president and secretary to the Board of Trustees. The semester opened with no serious problems, other than an unanticipated decline in our undergraduate enrollment. The administration attributed this to the unusually large number of students who earned their degree before the calendar change took place. Data showed that first-time-freshman enrollments had declined.

Race relations continued as a problem. A major dispute arose when Moses Turner announced that he would reduce the work week for employees in the Office of Minority Affairs to achieve an expected budget reduction. Why he chose that office and announced it to the media I do not understand. This obviously caused great concern to the staff and to the president. After intervention with the vice president by President Guyer, Moses Turner reversed the decision.

Following that event, Asian-American and Hispanic students had a confrontation with the Office of Minority Affairs over its alleged maldistribution of funds to the various minority student groups. African American students received a disproportionate amount of the funds. The numbers of Asian Americans and Hispanics on campus had grown significantly in the previous 10 years, but African Americans continued to be the largest minority group on campus. The amount of money at issue was small. Nevertheless, after meeting with Vice President Turner and the Office of Minority Affairs, the issue remained unresolved, and the situation escalated. Eventually, the Hispanic students formed a coalition with Asian Pacific Americans and made a major protest to President Guyer about the distribution of funds and a number of other matters. The lack of response to their concerns by the Office of Minority Affairs (OMA) had prompted the escalation. African American students, under the leadership of John Shapely and Isha Washington, did not join this protest, partly because they saw it as an attack against an African American administrator. This began a period of very poor relations among the various minority groups. The Hispanics and Asian Americans voiced their complaints at a Board of Trustees meeting.

President Guyer named a committee to review the students' concerns and, based on its findings, took two major actions. He removed the Office of Minority Student Affairs and the Office of Financial Aids from the administrative responsibility of the vice president for student affairs and services. These were assigned to Lee June, assistant provost for Student Academic Support Services and Racial, Ethnic, and Multicultural Issues. This move gave Lee June administrative responsibility not only for minority and handicapper students and issues relating to diversity, but also for the Office of Financial Aids, which affected all students and many units across the campus.

Race relations at MSU did not show any indication of improvement until spring 1993, when African Americans and Latinos assembled for a significant dialogue. Representatives of Asian Americans and Native Americans were present. The leaders of these groups knew one another and got along well. A new atmosphere may have begun, although the increase in Asian Americans and Hispanics at MSU could mean that more conflict with African Americans is likely in the future. Notably absent from this conference were white students. Until a real dialogue on race relations at MSU is established among all racial and ethnic groups, there will continue to be problems.

Later in the year, David Scott was named chancellor of the University of Massachusetts at Amherst. Also, Dean Richard Lewis resigned as dean of the Eli Broad College of Business; Harvey Sparks resigned as vice provost for health programs; John Tasker resigned as dean of the School of Veterinary Medicine; and Kathleen Bond resigned as dean of the College of Nursing. Judy Gentile, the pioneer in handicapper programs, died of cancer during the year, bringing to an end a significant era in MSU history. The next president of MSU, once selected, would need to make a number of important appointments. MSU entered the 1993 fall semester with many new challenges and opportunities confronting it.

▼

EPILOGUE

Statewide elections in 1992 changed the membership of the Board of Trustees. Democrats became the majority with the addition of Bob Traxler and Dorothy Gonzales—the first person of Hispanic background to serve on the board. I first met her in the late 1970s and was instrumental in bringing her to campus as a specialist.

Dorothy immediately took an active role in the MSU presidential search and selection, wanting it to be open rather than closed. The rest of the board took a different position. In 1993 the presidential search became embroiled in controversy when the Board of Trustees decided to keep it closed.

There was speculation on campus that David Scott would be a successful candidate for the MSU presidency. In 1993 all such speculation ended when Scott accepted the position at the University of Massachusetts; he had achieved his goal, and all wished him well.

Meanwhile, the names of more than 150 candidates for the presidency had been published in the *State News*. At the time, no one knew who released the list, which included names from on and off campus. I heard that the committee was actually working with a much smaller list, and this turned out to be the case. Within weeks it was announced that the names of four finalists would be submitted to the Board of Trustees. When a finalist from California withdrew, the candidates were: Dale Lick, president of Florida State University; Lou Anna K. Simon, interim provost at MSU; and

181

Henry Yang, engineering dean at Purdue University. Public interviews on campus were scheduled with the Council of Deans, faculty and students, the BFAA, the Minority Advisory Council, and the Board of Trustees. The interviews were well attended and I was present at all of them. Lou Anna Simon was interviewed first, Dale Lick second, and Henry Yang third.

Prior to the interview of Dale Lick, information was leaked to the press regarding racially insensitive remarks he had made about African American athletes. This created great difficulty for his candidacy. One trustee, Dorothy Gonzales, was quoted as being absolutely opposed to him. In his interview with the Council of Deans he directly addressed the issue, but at no time did he apologize or admit that he had made a major error. He did not respond adequately to the questions on this issue raised by Joe Darden, dean of Urban Affairs Programs, Dean Allen of James Madison College, and others. It was widely believed that Lick was preferred by a majority of the board, but once the controversy developed— and when his board chairman learned that he had applied for the MSU job without informing him, having been at FSU only two years—Lick withdrew after returning home. This left Lou Anna Simon and Henry Yang as the finalists.

When Yang appeared before the board, I attended and felt that, although he was an outstanding engineer, he did not seem adequately prepared for the presidential interview. At about this time I began to question the selection committee's motives, becoming convinced that they were not serious about either Simon or Yang and that they had wanted Lick all along. They were now left with a dilemma, compounded when Henry Yang returned to Purdue and notified the board he was withdrawing.

The Board of Trustees, under the chairmanship of Joel Ferguson, scheduled a public session to solicit advice from the MSU community. This meeting brought a large number of administrators, faculty, students, and others to the Lincoln Room in Kellogg Center. Most of those making presentations spoke in support of Simon's candidacy. At least two faculty were critical of the board, particularly the way it had sought to control the past president and run the university. Some trustees expressed reservations about the candidacy of an acting provost; some wanted a past or sitting university president to lead MSU. Eventually the Board of Trustees reopened the search.

Late in the summer the board suddenly announced on-campus interviews with a new candidate—M. Peter McPherson. Word spread rapidly about the interviews, which were held that day. The sessions went very well, and I was not surprised when, that same day, the board appointed him as the 19th president of Michigan State University. The future of MSU now rested with President Peter McPherson.

▼   ▼   ▼

President McPherson will have many issues to address at MSU, not the least of which is the financial situation. He made a good start by asking all deans, faculty, staff, and students to help him develop a set of principles and values to guide MSU during his presidency. In my opinion, four areas need his special attention:

1. minority/majority student relations,
2. undergraduate admissions,
3. undergraduate instruction, and
4. undergraduate student support services.

In one way or another, these have been areas to which I have devoted considerable time and energy for the last 25 years. I will offer here my own hopes and expectations of this new administration in these areas.

Minority/Majority Student Relations

To improve minority relations, MSU must move beyond the MSU IDEA to a new program that involves the diverse community of undergraduates. (The current program does not do this; the 1993 Latino conference attracted more students than did the entire MSU Diversity Conference.) Many speakers are brought to the campus for the Diversity Conference by various student organizations and by a host of academic departments and colleges. To improve this conference, visits with speakers need to be better coordinated, so that students have an opportunity to meet and interact with such guests as Anita Hill, Maya Angelou, and Charlene Hunter Gault.

In addition, it would help if the faculty would devote more attention to the speakers sponsored by students, as these are the programs at which student attendance is highest. If we can achieve better coordination in this area and greater linkage with classroom work, perhaps we can get beyond the kind of problems that arose when Minister Farrakhan visited MSU. Perhaps, too, we can move beyond the kind of crisis that arose in 1992 over the inequitable distribution of resources to minority student groups for funding programs.

Neither group—minority or white—has been prepared in high school for a multiracial and multicultural experience at MSU. The university also must recognize that minority student groups do not enter MSU ready for significant interaction with each other or with white students. Conversely, white students do not understand minority students and their diverse backgrounds (African Americans, Asian Americans, Hispanics, and Native Americans). If we want them prepared by the time they leave MSU, then we must plan with them ways of achieving this. Freshman year experience courses could contribute to a better orientation to the MSU community. A campuswide, year-long lecture series on multicultural issues and concerns could also help, but only if it is developed with diverse student groups. Also, discussion groups following each presentation would be essential. Differing points of view should be allowed. There is no doubt that forums should be available where dialogue on multiculturalism can and should occur, including in the living room or basement of Cowles House, to which the president could invite cross-cultural groups of student leaders.

Under no circumstances should MSU back away from its commitment to allow students to organize themselves along racial and ethnic lines. Such an effort would be unsuccessful in any case. Nor should the administration stop its support of Black caucuses,

Hispanic caucuses, and others, or eliminate the room set aside for these groups in the residence halls. Finally, the minority aide program should continue; and if this is not already closely coordinated with the resident aide program in the residence halls, it should be. Programming of activities in the halls by any group should be done for all students, not for any single group.

Undergraduate Admissions

Undergraduate admissions have gone well; enrollment levels have been maintained, and the number and percentage of minority students are increasing. Nonetheless, there are areas requiring attention. Each year the admission rate for African Americans lags behind those of Asian Americans and Hispanics, so that enrollments of African Americans—the largest minority group in Michigan—grow more slowly than for any other group. Many African Americans—often most—are still admitted under the College Achievement Admission Program (CAAP). Students so labeled are said to need academic support services, including remedial-development-preparatory (R-D-P) courses, yet many "regular admits" (mostly white) also need the same services. This situation needs correcting. Any student admitted to MSU who needs support services or R-D-P work in mathematics or writing should have access to such services through the colleges, departments, or Office of Supportive Services and Learning Resources Center. All CAAP students would cease to be labeled as such.

Undergraduate Instruction

When I came to MSU in 1968, instruction was much better handled by departments and faculty than it is today. In my own Department of Chemistry, the teaching of service courses was shared by all the faculty, and there was a coordinator of the freshman chemistry program. Laboratory demonstrations were a regular part of first-year courses. We lost all that in the mid-1970s and 1980s but have recently returned to it. Other departments and colleges have had similar experiences. Freshman students had access to small classes through the old university college departments, and this was a major feature of our recruitment program. Faculty now teach larger classes via the integrative studies centers. There is nothing wrong with large classes if they are done well by faculty who get sufficient support, but an adequate number of teaching assistants is hard, if not impossible, to obtain today. We must encourage a revitalization of quality instruction for our undergraduates. More faculty must return to teaching first-year and other undergraduate students, and they must be recognized for this by their faculty peers. But faculty will not do this with enthusiasm if they do not get support. Furthermore, graduate students should be used only in support of faculty, who should be the primary instructors. The practice in some academic units of having graduate students handle classes alone should stop. Foreign graduate students should acquire a thorough understanding of English before teaching our students.

Undergraduate Student Support Services

Michigan State University has had a long history of providing academic support to its students. It began in the early years with services designed by faculty and closely integrated with programs of study or courses taken by students. Typically, as with recitation sections, students received credit for the extra work they did in association with individual courses. This was not necessarily the case with respect to R-D-P courses, in which students commonly did extra work, spent extra time, and paid extra money but received no credit.

By the 1960s and early 1970s the university had expanded the number of underrepresented minority students (African American, Asian American, Hispanic, and Native American). Typically, they came from urban and rural areas less well endowed than suburban school districts, and MSU established a new generation of programs to serve their needs. These include the Office of Programs for Handicapper Students, the Office of Supportive Services, the Undergraduate University Division, the outreach efforts of Upward Bound and the Office of Precollege Programs (Talent Search and College Day), and many college-based and departmentally based programs, such as the College of Engineering's Equal Opportunity Program, the College of Natural Science's Drew/TAC Program, and The Eli Broad College of Business's Office of Minority Business Programs (which has been enhanced by additional funding from the Office of Minority Equity in the Michigan Department of Education). Today, MSU stands at a decisive point. The university can deliver academic support to most, but not all, of those undergraduates who need them. To meet the broader need, MSU must make changes in its academic support system.

For a university experiencing financial difficulties, as we are, the commitment of resources to student support services or to any other area is an important decision. I believe that despite diminished resources Michigan State University must continue to provide access to those services to underrepresented minority students and to majority students across the state who may need them. I would observe that support services must have a critical connection to courses or programs of study if they are to be relevant to the students' needs. Faculty must be involved in the development and/or implementation of academic support services for undergraduates at MSU, and means must be found to ease such involvement. This does not imply any expectation that most faculty will drop their research, instructional, and public service activities and take up new support service roles. On the contrary, only a few well-placed faculty in service departments (for example, American Thought and Language, Mathematics, Chemistry, Physics, Accounting, and the Centers for Integrative Studies) will take on this new challenge. That may be all that is needed. The presence of support services professionals has been crucial to the enrollment and retention of handicapper and minority students, particularly through the first year. They will also be crucial in the next phase—namely, as support to the faculty's efforts to design, set up, and deliver effective support services. I maintain that the academic support services professionals within the university must be retained, whether in the Undergraduate University Division, in Student Affairs and Services, a college, a school, or a department.

For too long, support services have not received the attention they should. Campuswide coordination has been partially achieved via the Supportive Services Advisory Committee to the Provost. This committee should be retained, but there should also be an Advisory Consultative Committee on Supportive Services.

The Undergraduate University Division has played a key role in academic support services. I noted earlier and will note again that the advising function remains a principal effort of this unit, which makes more than 28,000 contacts each year with both no-preference and major-preference students. Given that the number of no-preference students seldom exceeds 2,500, and allowing for duplicate or even triplicate contact with an individual student, these 28,000 contacts still mean that the UUD is doing a substantial portion of the advising of lower division major-preference students. Indeed, since this has been the pattern over several decades, I doubt that the colleges could take on these responsibilities. Thus, UUD must be maintained. In fact, the centralizing of other support units with UUD into space in Bessey Hall should be accelerated, and this includes moving the Office of Programs for Handicapper Students to a main floor site. To facilitate and give more visibility to the principal support role played by UUD, I think its director should be advised by a Lower Division Administrative Council of administrators, faculty, and students appointed by the provost. Analogous to the Teacher Education Council, it would consist of members of the staff of the college deans who are concerned with lower division matters. It would be chaired by the UUD director and include a representative from the Office of the Provost in an ex-officio capacity. Of course, none of this would be necessary if MSU had the equivalent of a college of sciences and the arts. No-preference students could easily be served within such a structure.

At some point the university's entire support services effort would benefit from the merger of the Office of Supportive Services and the Learning Resources Center. These two units now share facilities and collaborate in several areas. Their merger would result in a sharing of the best qualities of each and improved delivery of support services for undergraduates throughout the university. It is likely that both will continue to work with academic departments to build collaborative relationships with key faculty. The result could be a new unit strongly linked with the instructors in the departments, a linkage that has historically existed at MSU and at many other higher education institutions with learning centers.

I believe, furthermore, that it is in the best interest of MSU to have all university-level academic support programs under the provost. To that end, I propose that the academic support programs currently under the vice president for student affairs and under the director of intercollegiate athletics be placed under the provost.

▼   ▼   ▼

The issues I have identified may pale in comparison to other complex that will surely confront the new administration as time passes, but they may well be the very issues on which the future success of MSU will rest. Surely, research, graduate education, and public service activities will continue to be of paramount importance, and it is not my intention to diminish their place in the university's mission. I have tried to focus, however, on what I perceive to be important to the future of MSU and to the people of Michigan who send us their children to be educated.

▼

BIBLIOGRAPHY

Boyer, Ernest L. *College: The Undergraduate Experience in America.* New York: Harper and Row, 1987.

Hamilton, James B. "Concern for Academic Needs of the Disadvantaged." Office of Special Programs, Michigan State University, *Special Programs Bulletin*, vol. 1, no. 1, 1977.

———. "Interim Report on Retention of Enrolled Undergraduate Students." Office of the Provost, Michigan State University, 6 September 1983.

———. "Perspectives on Undergraduate Student Support Programs at Michigan State University: Past, Present and Future." Report to the Provost, Michigan State University, December 1991.

———. "Report on Special Programs." Office of the Assistant Provost for Special Programs, Michigan State University, 1973.

———. "Report on Special Programs." Office of the Assistant Provost for Special Programs, Michigan State University, 1974.

———. "Report on Special Programs." Office of the Assistant Provost for Special Programs, Michigan State University, 1975.

———. "Report to the National Science Foundation, Division of International Programs on the Results of a Visit to Nairobi, Kenya and Lagos, Nigeria." Office of the Assistant Provost for Undergraduate Education, Michigan State University, 1984.

———. "The Role of Professional Societies in Science and Technology for Development in Africa." In *Proceedings: African Regional Seminar on the Role of Scientific and Engineering Societies in Development*, 178-81. Washington, D.C.: American Association for the Advancement of Science, 1984.

―――. "Statement by Dr. James B. Hamilton Before the Subcommittee on Postsecondary Education." Statement presented to the U.S. House of Representatives, 11 April 1975.

―――. "Summary Proceedings of the Conference on Retention Sponsored by the Committee on Institutional Cooperation Held February 23-25, 1992 at Michigan State University." Prepared by James B. Hamilton for CIC located at the University of Illinois at Urbana, April 8, 1992.

―――. "The Synthesis and Characterization of Some Alkyl Sulfide Complexes of Niobium(IV)." Ph.D. diss., Iowa State University, 1968.

Hamilton, James B. and Robert E. McCarley. "Addition Compounds of Niobium(IV) Halides Formed with Monodentate Alkyl Sulfides: Synthesis, Spectra, and Magnetism." *Inorganic Chemistry* 9 (1970): 1333.

―――. "Addition Compounds of Niobium(IV) Halides and Zirconium(IV) Chloride Formed in 1,2-Dimethylthioethane: Synthesis, Spectra, and Magnetism." *Inorganic Chemistry* 9 (1970): 1339.

Henderson, Laura. "Open Rebuttal Report to the Third Annual Report of the Office of Special Programs." Office of Special Programs, Michigan State University, Fall 1975.

Kirksey, Kirby. "ESR Studies of 1,1-Dithiol Complexes with Niobium(IV)." Ph.D. diss., Michigan State University, 1975.

Madison Kuhn. *Michigan State: The First Hundred Years, 1855-1955.* East Lansing: Michigan State University Press, 1955.

McGinnis, Roger N. "Dimethyldithiophosphate Complexes of Niobium(IV) Tetrahalides." Ph.D. diss., Michigan State University, 1974.

Michigan State University. "Agenda, Michigan State University Black Parents Association, meeting held for Dr. John DiBiaggio." Michigan State University, 28 February 1989.

―――."Charge to the Assistant Provost for Special Programs." Office of the Provost, Michigan State University, 1971.

―――. "Coordinated Proposal: Recommendations to The Board of Trustees." Office of the President, Michigan State University, 22 March 1981.

————. "Implementation Memorandum #1, Office of the Provost Overview of the Implementation of CRUE Initiatives." Michigan State University, Council to Review Undergraduate Education, 21 November 1988.

————. "Implementation Memorandum #2, Office of the Provost, The CORE Program in the Knowledge Areas and the Emphasis Areas." Michigan State University, Council to Review Undergraduate Education, 20 February 1989.

————. "Implementation Memorandum #3, Office of the Provost, Admissions Policy and Entrance Requirements." Michigan State University, Council to Review Undergraduate Education, 17 November 1988.

————. "Implementation Memorandum #4, Office of the Provost, The Academic Governance System." Michigan State University, Council to Review Undergraduate Education, 14 July 1989.

————. "Implementation Memorandum #5, Office of the Provost, Writing." Michigan State University, Council to Review Undergraduate Education, 25 May 1989.

————. "Memorandum from President John DiBiaggio to Students Protesting in the Hannah Administration Building." 16 May 1989.

————. "Memorandum from Provost David K. Scott to Deans, Directors and Chairpersons, Regarding Legal Employment and Academic Status of Students Involved in Recent Sit-in the Hannah Administration Building." 17 May 1989.

————. "Modified Coordinated Proposal (Coordinated Proposal Modifications by Michigan State University, the Board of Trustees)." Office of the President, Michigan State University, 4 April 1981.

————. "Recommendations of President's Select Advisory Committee." Office of the President, Michigan State University, 1981.

————. "Report of the Committee of Sixteen, as adopted by the full committee." Office of the President, Michigan State University, 25 April 1968.

————. "Report of the Joint Committee on Writing Requirements, as approved by Academic Council." Joint Committee on Writing Requirements, Michigan State University, 8 January 1991.

————. "Report of the Task Force on Retention of Enrolled Undergraduate Students." Office of the Provost, Michigan State University, April 1982.

————. "Report to the President of the Commission on Admissions and Student Body Composition." Office of the President, Michigan State University, 1971.

————. "Report to the Provost from the Committee on Supportive Services for Minority Students and Students from Disadvantaged Backgrounds." Committee on Supportive Services for Minority Students and Students from Disadvantaged Backgrounds, Michigan State University, July 1979.

————. "Report to the Provost from the Women's Advisory Committee to the Provost on Affirmative Action." Women's Advisory Committee to the Provost on Affirmative Action, Michigan State University, 1986.

————. "Survey of Student Impressions of Life at Michigan State University, conducted for the Assistant Provost for Undergraduate Education by Dr. Susan C. Zonia." Social Science Research Bureau, Michigan State University, March 1989.

Vivio, Frank M. "Academic Support Services for Educationally Disadvantaged and Physically Handicapped Students: Results of a Survey of Michigan Postsecondary Institutions." Prepared at Michigan State University in the Office of the Assistant Provost for Special Programs in Cooperation with the Michigan Council of Equal Opportunity Programs. October 1975.

————. "Model for Evaluation of Programs for Students from Disadvantaged Backgrounds." Prepared in the Office of the Assistant Provost for Special Programs, Michigan State University, 1974.

Wilson, Bobby Lee. "The Synthesis and Characterization of Some Dihydrobis(pyrazol-1-yl)borate Complexes of Niobium(IV) and ESR Studies of Some Sulfur Donor Complexes of Niobium(IV)," Ph.D. diss., Michigan State University, 1976.

▼